MIRACULOUS, MAGICAL MOMENTS IN MINUTES

Over 500 Quick, Easy Activities
for Adults and Children to Share

Written and Photographed by

Becky B. Baxa

Hidden Splendor
Villa Ridge, MO

Published by Hidden Splendor, Villa Ridge, MO

Copyright 2012 by Becky B. Baxa, B.S., M. Ed.

Printed in the United States of America. 2012 All rights reserved.
The UPS Store, Jefferson City, Missouri: a veteran owned franchise business.

This book may not be reproduced in whole, in any form, or by any means, electronic or mechanical, including photocopying, recording, or by any information storage and retrieval system now known or hereafter invented, without written permission from the author.

If you would like to copy an activity or recipe (so your book doesn't get ruined) please feel free to do so. The hug and smile coupons, as well as the family activity calendar template, may be copied as many times as you need. Please give credit to the source when doing so.

This book is a collection of "odds and ends" ideas saved from the past 31 years of experiences. Many ideas are original and others have been modified, revised, "tweaked," and expanded by the author. There are also ideas presented in this book that are age old favorites handed down through the decades that should not be forgotten. Many activities have been used in workshops by the author for numerous years. The original source of some of these activities is unknown. Appropriate attribution will be made in future printings if the creators' identities become known.

Edited by Dottie Bodewitz, Mark Baxa, Jessica Hill, Dana Thomas and June Baker.
Graphics Contributor, Heather Kriete

Cover and photographs by Becky B. Baxa, supplemented with family archive photos.

Library of Congress control number: 2012902792

ISBN 978-0-9851565-0-3

A copy of this book may be ordered by contacting: hiddensplendor@ymail.com

Dedication

*"Whatever you do, whether in word or deed,
do it all in the name of the Lord Jesus,
giving thanks
to God the Father through Him."
Colossians 3:17*

Holy Bible, New International Version

Table of Contents

The purpose of this book..5
Why worry about the little things?...6
Tips to remember when doing activities with children..10
Family activity calendar..16

Activities..19
Hugs all around • 20 Hug license and coupon • 21 Variety of ways to praise your child • 22 Smile coupon • 24 The family dinner table • 25   A child's perspective • 28 Meal presentation = fun • 30 Meal planning and food fun • 34 Read! • 39 Building family unity • 42 Daily question • 43 Leave a message • 45 The ties that bind us…• 46 Puzzles • 47 Guessing games • 53 Matching games • 56 Lace-up cards • 60 Puppets • 61 Music • 66 Hand and foot fun • 68 Mirror, mirror on the wall • 70 Dress up – dramatic role playing • 71 Carpet and yarn • 77 Newspaper fun • 78 Exploration • 79 Construction • 80 Long time favorites • 83 Body challenges • 89 Balloons • 94 Flash light fun • 96 Fishing pond • 97 The magic of bath time • 98 Pretend to be...• 99 Card board boxes • 101 Cardboard tubes • 104 Packing materials • 105 Milk carton magic • 106 On the road again... • 107 Pets! • 108 The senses • 111 Discovery • 113 Prediction • 116 Observation • 117 Counting • 119 Count the change • 120 Clocks/telling time • 121 Fractions • 122   Measuring • 123   Shapes • 124 Where in the world...geography • 125 Neighborhood map/vehicle play mat • 126 Writing • 127 Letters • 128 This and that • 129

The Four Seasons..130
Winter • 131 Treats for the birds • 133 Spring • 134 Summer • 135 Sand • 142 Water • 143 Bubbles • 146 Butterflies • 147 Fall/Autumn • 149 Nature anytime of the year • 152 The weather • 153

Arts/Crafts..154
Paper chains • Book markers • Gift tags • Rubbings • Draw a cartoon • 154 Draw a made up creature! • Create made up faces • Three-way creature creations book • Stick people • 155 Stencils • Aluminum foil sculptures • 156 Body outlines • Fingerprint creatures • Necklace • Collage • Label design • 157 Clay sculptures • Homemade play dough • Surprise play dough balls • Candy cane art • Slime /finger paint • Silly putty • 158 Fold a fan • Swirling Colors • 159 Mix colors • Magic slates/corn syrup bags • Bleach drawing • Marble painting • 160 Potato prints • String painting • Mirror image printing • Water colors • Coffee filter butterflies • 161

Recipes..162
Fruit sparkle ice cubes • Homemade applesauce • 163 Fun food ideas • 164 Graham cracker house • 165 Royal icing • 167 Ziploc® pastry bag • 168 Peanut butter play dough • 169 How to color rice and pasta • 169 Bubbles • Play dough • 170 Silly putty • Cornstarch clay • 171 Feely box • 172 Newspaper hat or boat • 173 Swirling colors • Magic slate • 174 Erupting volcanoes • 175 Wave bottles • 176

Your Ideas..177
Resources..178
Epilogue..179

THE PURPOSE OF THIS BOOK

Explore ideas that are quick and easy to reconnect adults and children in a society of frazzled, on-the-go families. This book can be used by parents, grandparents, relatives, babysitters, child care providers, preschool and early elementary school teachers.

The concept of the ideas you now hold began about 15 years ago when I was asked to speak at a Family and Consumer Sciences Conference in Ames, Iowa. I was told to come up with something about quick, easy activities to do with children. As a spin-off from a workshop I had created 10 years before, <u>Miraculous, Magical Moments in Minutes</u> was developed.

Since that time many ideas have been added to the workshop and presented to a variety of groups in various forms. I'm sure this is not the end of the story. There are many more ideas to be enjoyed. Hopefully, the 500 plus ideas that follow in this book will jump start your creativity. Have fun, enjoy, and start building your memory quilt!

Quilt made by author's Great Grandma Clara Pepperdine Baker
and Great Aunt Nanny Ward.

WHY WORRY ABOUT THE LITTLE THINGS?

Take a moment to think back to your childhood. Which memories stand out in vivid color, with joy, in your memory bank?

Ask your spouse, parents, friends and adult family members. What do they remember as their most fun, happy times? Write them down and then evaluate what type of experiences brought all of these people pleasant memories.

I remember one magical moment from my youth when an adult and I…

When my husband smells chicken soup it brings back vivid memories for him. He faithfully tells me about his great grandmother who lived upstairs when he was a small boy. He fondly remembers sneaking up to share a bowl of soup with her and basking in her undivided attention.

I remember a time staying with a lady one evening when my parents had gone out. We spent the evening searching her bedroom for the sparkling sequins that had fallen off of her night cap! After we had collected a substantial amount of "treasure," we made a new dress for the doll I had brought that evening.

Many childhood afternoons were spent under a blanket thrown over the clothesline at my mother's knee while she hung laundry or under a blanket bearing card table while the garden was being weeded. Together we created a fantasy world that filled the air with delight and wonder.

What did your memories look like? I would venture to guess most of your memories did not cost a lot of money or take a lot of time. The best way to show children you love, appreciate, and respect them, or make them feel special, is by spending time with them. Children need to be acknowledged, looked at, smiled at, and hugged… every day!

What a simple thing to do! Have you actually looked at and made eye contact with your child today? Have you smiled at them? Given a hug? Had a conversation where you actively listened with your eyes as well as your ears? Too many times parents and adults are overworked, filled with stress, pressures, and their own personal pursuits that they end up only giving directions and commands to their children each day. Parents are tired and wondering how to get off of life's human hamster wheel.

We do not know what tomorrow holds. The future is not ours. For this fact we need to be determined to live today and everyday as if it was our last. We should live so that tomorrow there will be no regrets.

It was July 2007. I had been working with a ten year old special needs homebound child for several years. She had become very ill, spent weeks in a coma and then died. I was traveling into town four days after her funeral when the call came in. My husband told me to pull off the road. My son had been in an accident and had broken his leg. I was instructed to go about my errands and they would meet me at home. Twenty minutes later another call told me to get to the hospital as quickly as possible (almost an hour's drive) and that things looked bad. While working at a repair shop, our son had been struck by a race car that was being repaired that day. As the car entered the bay, the driver's foot slipped off the clutch, slamming my son's body into a wall. Both legs were smashed. Ten days later after intensive care, a ventilator, pneumonia and two surgeries we came home to face four months of recovery and therapy. I was his home health care nurse…a job I was not very good at! Arriving home, the refrigerator and water softener broke, and the ordered downstairs carpet finally arrived with a hole smack dab in the middle. Things were a mess and seemed bleak.

Within a few weeks time, my job changed and our finances were stretched. I was mourning the death of a treasured student. I went from being a home-bound teacher to a home health care aide. My son went from being healthy and working, to disabled. Thankfully, he is walking today; but it was a long road to recovery that still has side effects.

You see, life can change in a minute. One phone call, one event, a split second accident…you do not know what the future holds. All the more reason to make the most of each minute you are blessed with in this life!

Have you ever walked through the grocery store, sat in a parking lot or restaurant and watched the people? If you have, you may be shocked to see how many are focused on the electronic devices they have in front of them instead of the people beside them. Let me give you an example. I watched a couple having lunch together at a restaurant. I say this very loosely. The entire time they ate their meal, not once did the couple speak to each other! They were each working on a computer and there was no interaction. Several times one would get up to get something from the beverage center, but even then, they did not speak to each other. Eventually, they packed up and left the restaurant.

Many times I jokingly accuse my husband of the "third" person in the room with us. I tease him until he, with embarrassment or excuses, puts the device away. Technology is a big part of today's world.

In the "hamster wheel" of daily life are you guilty of going through routines while communicating on an electronic device without looking at, talking to, or listening to your children?

If you get nothing else from this book, please remember to create meaningful, magical, memorable memories with your children by smiling, hugging, and communicating with them each and every day. In this book you will find many ideas to try, and to "spring board" off of to create magical moments with your children. There will be a variety of ideas presented across many areas of interest and ages. They also vary in the amount of time, preparation and supplies you will need. Always keep in mind your child's age and developmental stage, modifying and adapting the activities as needed.

Before you move on, try this experiment. Set a timer for one minute (or have someone watch the second hand on a watch to help you). Just sit or stand (don't peek!) and experience what a minute feels like. Take note of when you think the minute is over. Was it longer than you thought it would be? Most people say "YES!"

Brainstorm ideas of what you could have done with your child in that minute. How many things can you think of? It can be as simple as counting with them, singing a song or counting how many seconds it takes the light to change to green.

Pretty impressive, huh?

We often think that quality time takes too much quantity of time, effort or even money!

But, if you remember back to your most pleasant childhood memories, they probably didn't involve the big things. You might have remembered the little, simple, uncomplicated, consistent interactions with the adults you love. It was the little pieces you saved and treasured that produced the beautiful memory quilt of your life.

I've had a quote above my desk for years. I believe it fits perfectly at this point. This is what it says:

> *"Our greatest danger in life is in permitting the urgent things to crowd out the important."* —*Charles E. Hummel*

Before planning those first magical moments, let's look at some tips in the next chapter to make your time run more smoothly and pleasant.

TIPS TO REMEMBER WHEN DOING ACTIVITIES WITH CHILDREN

1. Look for fun and often teachable moments! Be spontaneous and don't be afraid to act silly. Kids will love it! Ask children how many different things they can think of to do with an item. Then "go with the flow." For example: a round yogurt container can scoop sand or water, pour beans, be used to trace around (usually a large circle and a smaller circle) it can hold crayons or other treasures, you can cut the bottom out of it and use it for a megaphone; several with lids can be used for stacking, sorting or storing.

2. Plan ahead. A project calendar is a fun way to get the children involved and excited with anticipation plus help you plan ahead. You can make your own or use a prepared one, like the one in this book on page 17.

3. Be prepared! If you have pre-planned an activity gather all the materials you need before you start. Getting started and then finding out you are missing a needed item will produce disappointment or you will lose your "audience's" attention and interest while you locate the materials. It is like popping the magic "bubble."

4. Be consistent in creating magical moments each day. Illnesses, unplanned events, vacations, holidays, oversleeping, etc. may interrupt your routine. This is part of life and can be used in itself as a teaching moment about flexibility, adapting, disappointment, etc. It may be the perfect prelude to one of those heart-to-heart moments building character in your child. Just having a one-on-one, undivided attention conversation will be a magical moment in itself.

5. Safety is number one! Make sure the activities you plan are developmentally and age appropriate! Projects that are not for your child's age and developmental stage may be dangerous. Ben Franklin's saying that "An ounce of prevention is worth a pound of cure" still stands true today. Do activities with your children! Wise judgment and supervision are critical. None of the projects in this book are dangerous if done with supervision and at the correct developmental stage. Besides, how can you interact with your child if you are not doing the activity with them?

6. Modify and adapt activities to meet your child at their developmental stage. If you think an activity looks fun, but your child is not old enough or is too old for that particular activity, what can you do to modify it to make it safe, interesting, fun and challenging? Learning numbers one through ten is fun for a three year old. Learning numbers up to millions and billions would be fun for older children. Once my fourth grader used our home copy machine to make a million dollars. He wanted to know what a million dollars would look like. It took him days and hours of counting. In the end he put his "million dollars" in one of his dad's old brief cases and pretended to be a business owner conducting big deals. He wrote out contracts and bills of sale. He is 22 years old today. And, guess what? He owns his own business!

7. Laughter is the best medicine! If a project doesn't turn out as expected keep your sense of humor and ham it up. The kids will love it and it may be their favorite memory!

You know…something like this: It was the late 90's. The scene was set. I was to document on film this momentous occasion. My oldest son was the news announcer covering the event. My youngest and his dad were the scientist and launch safety specialist. I was assured that where I stood was the safest place to stand. I asked several times even. The cardboard tube rocket shot straight up, we began to cheer. Then it did a U-turn and within inches buzzed swiftly by my ear! It is to this day the most remembered launch! I got "in trouble" for not catching the whole flight on film!

8. Use activities as a learning tool for you! If you listen very closely during your child's play you will discover what makes them "tick." This will be magnified during role playing or any time they are using their imagination. It is during this time that you will want to make great mental lists. These lists will provide you with direction on what activities to provide in the future, what areas need to be worked on, encouraged, or reinforced. During play you often will discover your child's worries, fears, strengths, interest, talents, and blossoming virtues.

My boys, when they were young, did a lot of role playing. When their daddy traveled internationally for weeks at a time, they would set up ticket windows on a TV tray and cardboard conveyor belts rolling suitcases over them, playing airport. Their play indicated their thoughts and worries. So we listened to pre-recorded stories read by their daddy, we marked the calendar for his return and checked off each day, we marked a map with dots on the places he would visit, we talked about what daddy was doing each day and we explored the many jobs and services provided by airports.

My husband was greatly upset when I brought home my old kitchen set for the boys to play with. It didn't help that it was pink! I know…I painted it white. He had a stereotyped view that this was for girls. The boys did not disappoint me though, as they set up espresso and cappuccino shops and charged me exorbitant amounts of play money for each cup! We exchanged pretend money and counted change. They would take turns being the customer and the employee behind the counter making the day's creations. Both boys are in business today.

In my Sunday school class of four year olds, we were cutting out figures for a dramatic role play backdrop. I noticed one little boy struggling. He held the scissors like a flower bouquet and didn't know where to put his fingers. I made a special note to let him have more cutting time. Activities give clues on how we can encourage and improve our child's development.

I had a friend once tell me after her son's preschool evaluation that he could not cut paper. After some conversation I realized that that was the first time her son had ever held scissors. She said they weren't safe. Well, to a point. But, preschool children need to work on fine motor skills. With the use of blunt scissors and supervision, scissor time can be a wonderful time. Let your child sit with an envelope (even from your junk mail, they won't care) or let them cut out pictures they like from an appropriate magazine. Put the child's name on the envelope and it can become their special collection of pictures. They will be thrilled. Or, as you sort mail, have them sit with you and just cut up the mail you are going to throw out. The more they cut, the better control they will have of their fine motor skills, making writing and tying their shoes or holding a knife to cut meat, etc., easier when it is time.

9. Documentation allows the activity to be enjoyed over and over again. One winter, my youngest (when he was in about second grade) rigged up a pulley system through my kitchen island light. We tied a pinecone on the yarn suspended through the pulley. He hoisted it up and over to his Granny, who smeared the pinecone with peanut butter. Next the pinecone traveled to the bird seed bowl into which it was plunked. The resulting creation was repeated over and over until our bag of pinecones was empty. We then took our masterpieces outside and decorated a tree in the back yard for the birds. We took many pictures of this endeavor. The pictures were poured over repeatedly and this activity remained a tradition for many years until the boys reached high school. See page 133.

Fun memories can be relived repeatedly if documented in photos. Younger children can dictate to an adult and older children can write and/or tell stories in a journal. Taking photos, keeping a journal, writing stories and video recording are all ideas to document your activities. Preserving those priceless, magical moments will never be regretted!

Scrapbooking can take on many forms besides the traditional version. For example: A spiral notebook (or an old book) can be one way to document activities. Decorate the front with a title. Fill the pages with photos and captions about your activities. Use construction paper, colored paper, stickers, etc. to help decorate the pages. Let children write their names and dates on each page. They can even think up captions for the photos and if old enough write in the journal themselves. Printing off pictures from your computer, slipping them into plastic sleeves, and then into a three ring binder is another option.

10. Make clean up part of the activity! I frequently told my children that if we all cleaned up together, whether it be a current activity or dinner dishes, that there would be more time to play together later. Cleaning up can be fun! There are many clean up songs available. It would be fun to make up your very own personal family clean up song. Let the kids be the composers. Cleaning up together teaches responsibility, accountability, cooperation, and minimizes the mess. It also helps the adult feel more like making a mess if they know there will be co-operation and support during the clean up process.

- Insist that children put back activities with parts and pieces. Have a place for everything and make sure everything is in its place at the end of the day or play time. Labeling boxes with names and pictures for non-readers and shelves the same way, makes picking up a matching game. This helps with the clean up process.

- Smaller children need to have the cleaning process broken down into steps small enough for them to succeed. Guidance, direction, patience and supervision are also needed by an adult until a child masters this skill. Remember a child's attention span is much shorter than an adult's. And the adult mind wanders every three minutes! Just imagine how many times a child's mind flitters off to another thought process.

- So instead of saying "clean up" now. Break it into steps. For example: I'll clean the paint brushes while you pick up all the paper. Or you pick up all the cars and trucks and I'll roll up the play mat.

Author's story: I remember my babysitter telling us to clean up the toy room. She would suggest this numerous times at escalating levels of volume. She never went into the room to help us. It was more of a stern, exasperated command. We would always obediently go into the toy room and start. The day would drag on and we would play. The adult voice from the kitchen would continue to remind us of our purpose. We knew exactly what elevation level of her voice meant we needed to get down to business. At that point we would literally shove all the toys, packed tightly as we could, under the bed!

As the voice became louder approaching the room for the final warning, we would perch angelically on the edge of the bed and smile. She would nod and go back to her cooking. The next morning when I would arrive at the babysitter's house, all the toys were back on the shelves in their correct spots. She must have re-done the clean-up job each night. Now I have two thoughts about this. First of all, she created a whole lot of extra work for herself. A little time spent teaching and guiding us through the task of how she wanted the toys put away would have been worth the time and saved her a lot of frustration. It would have avoided the long drawn out process while she waited for us to do the job she expected to be done. Applying this principle with your children will be helpful.

My second thought is that when you give a child a task to do on their own, accept their results and praise their efforts. Like the first time I allowed my child to dress without any help (at his insistence). He came out in shorts and shirt that were put on backwards and different colored socks. That is the way we went proudly to town that day. We were quite the pair, one beaming child and one slightly embarrassed parent. We both lived through the experience.

- Store supplies and games you have made in nice containers. They should be labeled and decorated. Image is important to a child's perception of the value and care they place on the use of items. Consider decorative boxes or tins, or food containers that have been relabeled in a creative way. This sends a silent message to children that what is inside is special and they need to be careful with it.

- What items you store together also silently tells children how to behave. Airplanes and cars with the books and puzzles? One activity says zoom and run around. The other activity says let's sit and have a quiet time. Think about the silent messages you are sending your children.

> By creating an environment of playful laughter and dazzling discoveries, you receive a vast array of miraculous moments! These precious, treasured minutes build family unity; and builds stronger, warmer, happier relationships in which children are willing and ready to laugh with and trust adults. These times decrease the generation gap as you increase your knowledge about each child, resulting in brighter, more intelligent, broader minded children.

FAMILY ACTIVITY CALENDAR

Everyone likes to look forward to things. A family activity calendar is a great way to help plan ahead and make sure you can think of something special to do each day. Fun activities during the day can also encourage your children to think about things, act on inspirations or new-found interests, ask questions or continue to learn more about a subject.

Anytime of the day that works for you is ideal. Remember your experiment with a minute? It doesn't have to be a large scheduled block of time to slip in a magical moment. Be spontaneous, but consistent each day. Remember though, if you miss once or twice the earth will not stop spinning. My guess is once you have started and have made this a habit in your daily routine, your kids won't let you forget to check the calendar for their special time and activity with you! Keep in mind, it really isn't so much what you do, it is more about having you all to themselves with undivided time.

In the following pages you will find a list of things to do with your children. There are thousands of more ideas out there. This is just to get you started. Be creative. Pick your favorite and add them to your family calendar. Some may stretch over several days or require a little pre-planning.

If age appropriate, have a family meeting and read through the list noting the activities that spark interest. Then fill in your monthly calendar. You might want to throw in some surprises too. Pick activities that will help encourage your child's development and foster their interests.

Remember to evaluate all activities for age and developmental appropriateness. An activity that is meant for an older child may be unsafe and cause frustration. Use good judgment and modify and adapt activities to your child's level of development. The activity should be just hard enough to be challenging, encouraging them on to the next level; yet not so difficult that you produce frustration or lack of interest.

FAMILY ACTIVITY CALENDAR

Month:　　　　　　　　　　Year:

Sunday	Monday	Tuesday	Wednesday	Thursday	Friday	Saturday

PLEASE REMEMBER...

The following activities are a random sampling of ideas that cover many areas of interest and ages.
They vary in time, preparation, and supplies required.
Always
keep your child's age and stage of development in mind before doing an activity.
Modify
as needed for your child's skills.

Use good judgment.

Safety and supervision must always be a priority!

Spend some time today interacting with your family instead of watching a TV show or playing on the computer.

ACTIVITIES

How many ways
can I show you
I love you…

Let me count the ways…

HUGS ALL AROUND

Hugs...there is so much to say about hugs! Hugging is good for people. It makes both people feel better. One size fits all, it uses little energy but gives a huge power boost! Hugs help relieve tension, reduce stress, help you relax and feel loved. They fight depression and loneliness. Hugs make you beam with a raised self esteem. They are free with no negative side effects. They don't require batteries or check-ups and are available in endless supply. Hugs are chemical free, naturally sweet, and are 100 percent wholesome.

Have you ever noticed the "huggy" people in your lives always find the positive and seem to be filled with more joy? Without a doubt, hugs generate good will, open up feelings of being connected, safe and accepted. A hug might possibly be the best "medicine" you can get or give each day.

So, your miraculous moment is to give hugs! Hugs in the morning, hugs in the noon time, hugs in the evening, hugs at bedtime. HUGS! It is a precious moment that will create magical memories for both the giver and the receiver! So go hug someone! Never hug tomorrow someone you can hug today.

On the next page you will find examples of hug coupons. Make your own, or copy these, and pass them out. Children love to get these. They can save them for a time when they need a hug and you don't notice first. Then, of course, when presented with the coupon, stop and redeem the value immediately! That's a great door opener for a conversation too! Walk through that opportunity door and get to know your loved one better.

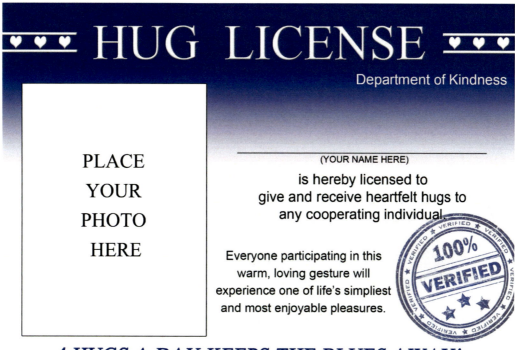

A VARIETY OF WAYS TO PRAISE YOUR CHILD!

WOW
Way to go
Super
You sure are special
Outstanding
Excellent
Great
Good
Neat
Well done
Remarkable
I knew you could do it
I'm PROUD of you
Fantastic
Super star
Beautiful
Nice work
Looking good
You're on top of it
Positively 100%
Beautiful
Now you're flying
You're spectacular
You are important
You tried hard
You make me happy
You've got a friend
You make me laugh
You brighten my day
I respect you
That's correct
You're a JOY
You're a treasure
You're wonderful

You're catching on
Now you've got it
You're incredible
Bravo
You're fantastic
Hurray for you
You're on target
Nice
Terrific
How smart
Good job
That's incredible
Hot dog
Dynamite
You're beautiful
You're unique
Bingo
Good for you
I like you
You're a winner
Remarkable job
Beautiful work
Spectacular
You care
That's perfect
Awesome
A+ job
You're OK
My buddy
You made my day
That's the best
Give them a hug
A giant kiss
Fantastic job

You're darling
You're precious
Great discovery
You've discovered the secret
You figured it out
Fantastic job
Hip, hip, hurray
Nothing can stop you now
Magnificent
Marvelous
You're on your way now
You mean the world to me
Phenomenal
Exceptional
You're a real trooper
You're real responsible
You learned it right
You are exciting
What an imagination
What a good listener
You are fun
You're growing up
Beautiful
You are important
You mean a lot to me
Say, I LOVE YOU!
A nod, smile combo

A SMILE!

EYE CONTACT
with all of the above!

Go through the list and mark your favorites.
Can you think of your own to add?

Somehow it always seems that we use the same phrases. I didn't believe this, until one year when I was teaching high school my picture appeared in the Year Book. It was a photo of me with a huge smile... so far so good... my hand raised in apparent delight... again, so far so good and then the caption... "Wonderful! Wonderful!!". It was then that I realized, that phrase was used BY ME for everything that pleased me. I dug out a list of ways to praise your child that I used when teaching self esteem. I began to explore other ways to praise my students and my children. What is your favorite "praise phrase?" Do you mix them up or do you have a catch-all. I challenge you to expand your horizons and think of more ways than on the list. I know you will do "wonderfully!"

I especially liked the last way... to SMILE! Smiles are such an amazing, wonderful thing. It doesn't cost anything, you never run out of them when giving them away and you never tire of receiving them. If you give one away you are not more poor. Yet if you get a smile you are somehow richer, boosting you up and filling you with happiness. A smile only takes a minute, but the memory of that smile may last a lifetime. The amazing thing about smiles is that when you give one away, it somehow makes you feel just as happy as the person you gave it to. A smile tells someone that you like them, that you are friends, it communicates good will and acceptance. A smile makes the home a happier place to be and business more pleasant. A simple smile cheers you up, pushes away sadness or fears, gives encouragement and makes pain and trouble a whole lot easier to deal with. You can not buy a smile or steal one. A smile has no value at all until it is given freely and lovingly away or until it is received. What an amazing, simple action. Yet it carries such a huge value!

Why not give some smiles away today? Your happiness tank will be filled as you fill-up the tanks of those around you! It has been said that a smile is worth a THOUSAND words! Proverbs 17:22 (NIV) says: "A cheerful heart is good medicine, but a crushed spirit dries up the bones." A smile is like good medicine. It makes us cheerful. Even if you don't really "feel" like smiling, if you try it for awhile, most of the time, you begin to feel happier as a result. It will make people wonder what you have been up to.

Make some smile coupons and give them to your children. Use them to help ease stressful situations, during trials and disappointments. Could you stay upset if your child pulled out a coupon and handed it to you? Do you think you might get a smile from a sad child if you presented a coupon out of your pocket especially for them? You don't even need a physical coupon. Every parents pockets can be filled with an endless supply of smiles to share with children at a needed time. Just reach inside your pocket, pretend to dig deep looking for the perfect smile and "ta-da!" pull out their uniquely designed smile just for them!

Give it a try! Here is an example.

THE FAMILY DINNER TABLE

The light dimmed as we descended the stairs. I could feel the cool damp air on my skin. I looked around in anticipation. It was then that my eye stopped and stared. It sat looking forlorn and unloved with skin peeling in unsightly patches, cast away like a worn out slipper. Four tired companions stayed close, standing in silent loyalty. Parts hung and dangled, yet held strong in a valiant effort to maintain dignity.

I sighed, as a thousand memories flashed through my mind of the time we had spent together. I made arrangements to bring this old friend home. Home to a place where it would be honored for the many magical memories it had enabled.

What I brought home that day was my parent's old kitchen table. We ate dinner at that table almost every night for as long as I can remember. This table was the nerve center of my childhood home. It was a place for communication. The mail pile always sat to the left side. It was the location for teaching, counseling, visiting, as well as eating. It was at that table that we discussed our day's activities, made family plans, made decisions and talked out delicate situations. This table was the place where business transactions were made, homework was done, crafts were made, letters were written, books were read, celebrations and even tea parties took place. It was a favored spot to do almost any activity in the Winter, as it had a forced air heat register below it that would warm your feet. Yes, this table was the central meeting spot for the heart of my home.

As I searched for a picture of this table, I became frustrated to find so many photos of the dining room table, not the kitchen table! The dining room table was used for the really big occasions and holidays. Yet, I have no fond memories of that table. I wondered why?

Then as if a shade had been opened and the sunlight streamed through, I knew it wasn't the table or the big occasions that created the fond memories. It was the little things, the daily consistency of family unity, that composed the magical memories. Like scraps of a quilt, each piece telling a story, all sewn together into one big beautiful quilt.

> Coming together as a family each day, communicating with one another, talking and listening, is a powerful tool that makes families stronger!

I thought again about this table for which I held such a powerful fondness. It was silly really, after all it was just a table. But, it was the memories it rekindled, and the spirit of family that it represented, that made it special. My grandfather's handprints are on the bottom of all four chairs. One time when he repainted the table he carried the chairs with wet hands off to dry.

I wondered, ...if that table could talk, or if it had kept a diary, what would it say? This table had been won by my father's mother (my Grandma Baker) in a grocery store raffle drawing. I'm not sure what year that was. My grandparents were married in 1927. A picture was found of an unidentified family member taken in 1944 sitting on one of the chairs. We can conclude that the brand new table set arrived sometime in that time frame.

1944 photo of an unidentified relative sitting on one of the chairs

My mom and dad were married in 1950 and the table and chairs went with them to set up "housekeeping." I lived at home for 21 years and then the table joined my family in 2000. We now have the fifth generation sitting around this table making memories.

It really doesn't matter what activity you do with your children. Just do something! Spending time with your children, effectively communicating with them, is possibly the greatest gift you could offer.

So, you could stop reading this book right now…take what you have read so far, (smile, hug, communicate) EVERY DAY and you will have a great success rate of making magical memories with your children. But, please don't stop, there are lots of great ideas ahead!

These photos show generations in action using the old white table.

A CHILD'S PERSPECTIVE

Think about the view of the world from a child's perspective. Try crawling around your kitchen, living room or bedroom and take a look at what your children see. Are you surprised?

What if we were forced to sit in a chair in which our feet dangled, or stuck straight out? What if at every meal someone tied a huge bib around our neck and gave us a large mixing bowl and big metal spoon to eat with? How hard would it be for you to sit in a contented state and be happy if this were so?

Think about your children. What can you do to make things just the right size for them?

For years we had a small table in the center of our kitchen. Many times, if my husband was traveling, the boys and I ate our dinner together at their little table, not the regular size adult table. After all, the little people outnumbered the adults when dad was traveling.

I also cleaned out a drawer in the kitchen, at their level, and filled it with table activities. This drawer contained water colors, brushes, paper, stencils, crayons, colored pencils, construction paper, child scissors, glue sticks, play dough and silly putty. All of these activities could be supervised while cooking and we could have a conversation while both occurred. Often we played together during the day and before or after meal time. Many fond memories were made around that little table, which is now in my son's kitchen working magic for a new generation.

No matter what size table it is, memories are still made around them. This little table pictured below (made for me by my Grandpa Baker when I was two years old) is now on its third generation."

Becky, age 2   Becky's son   Becky with grandson

> Providing child size equipment shows respect to our children. Remember children's dinnerware and infant, toddler and youth size flatware too.

MEAL PRESENTATION = FUN

- Mealtime can be a time for special memory making. Any day can become a special day with just a few additions. Celebrate the arrival of Spring, the first day of school, loosing a tooth, finally being able to tie a shoe, and so forth.

- My mom had a flare for "fancying" up a meal. In college I learned that color was the key to meal planning. Whatever you add, remember the little touches DO make a difference. A candle stuck in the morning's waffle, a tiny paper umbrella added to a glass, let your imagination be your guide.

- One meal from childhood stands out in my memory. It consisted of fried bologna, filled with instant mashed potatoes. A spoon created an indentation in the potatoes in which peas were added as pretend eggs to the make believe "bird's nest." Now this is not particularly a gourmet meal. But when my mom presented it in this fashion I thought we were dining like royalty!

- This idea always elicited giggles and groans (at Mom's silliness) from my kids. Serve an April Fool's meal by trying some crazy things. Float plastic eye balls in your drink. Plant plastic spiders in the mashed potatoes or rolls. Serve dinner food at breakfast, like macaroni and cheese, or meatloaf muffins "iced" with mashed potatoes and decorated with carrot stick candles (pictured on the left below). Tape down silverware and make sure they don't match. Colored plastic ware works well. Give everyone a different kind of chair, plate and glass. Decorate the center of the table with a "flour" bouquet (bag of flour). Wear clothes inside out or some crazy combination.

- Another popular hit was born out of a misunderstanding. My pre-kindergartener came home from school moaning. He could not understand why no one remembered his half birthday. They had celebrated it at school that day because he had a summer birthday. Not even his granny remembered. He was crushed! Hence, the half-birthday party was born.

    Ideas for a half-birthday party: Cut a paper plate in half, serve half a sandwich, half a piece of fruit and half a glass of milk. Cut a birthday card in half and have fun! There are no gifts on half birthdays. The celebration was the gift.

- Surprise Milk – after pouring a glass of milk, add some chocolate or strawberry syrup. Do not stir it. Let your child be surprised as they stir the milk to discover the flavor.

- Big or small, make meals special with the little touches.

- Valentine's Day all in red and lace (pictured on the left.) St. Patrick's Day with green Jell-O®, green drink, Irish stew and "blarney stone" rolls (pictured on the right).

- Special touches: Food coloring in a glass of milk, special napkins, a balloon here or there, a special note at each place written on a paper napkin, candle light, use the good dishes, foods made in special pans (you don't have to use them just for cake or Jell-O®), a homemade banner, party hats, themed food (all one color or all round).

- One time the dining room table was set with the nicest dishes, napkins and a centerpiece. The kids asked who was coming for dinner. I told them it was a surprise and someone very special. At dinner time I announced that they were the special guests!

- Eat in different settings…eat outside under a tree or at a picnic table, have a picnic on a blanket in the flower garden, on the porch, in a tent (in or outside), in a tree, in the hayloft or garage, at a park, while camping.

- Children love to play restaurant and serve meals to their family. My son would put on an apron, add a towel over his arm and talk in a funny voice. One day I found him a tuxedo t-shirt to wear while serving. He loved it!

- Use cookie cutters to cut bread slices into fun shapes. Stars, hearts, dinosaurs…then make them into sandwiches.

- While making pancakes, use a measuring cup with a pour spout for the batter and pour shapes onto the griddle. A pig, mouse, snowman, etc. Make some mystery shapes and let the children decide what they are! Let children pour the batter to make their own shapes. Smaller children will need supervision.

MEAL PLANNING AND FOOD FUN

- Make and decorate sugar cookies. Cut them into fun shapes.

- Make cookie care packages for someone outside your family to brighten their day.

- Make a graham cracker house with an empty cardboard carton underneath. Decorate your house with an assortment of cereals and candy. See recipe on page 165.

- As children get older let them plan and prepare (with supervision) a meal and then serve it to the family.

- Measuring Matters - How many teaspoons are in a tablespoon? How many teaspoons are in a half or one cup? Get out the measuring spoons, cups, water, and start experimenting.

- Bake a cake together. Let the kids decorate it using different color icing and decorations. Make sure you praise their efforts, have a photo shoot and of course eat their creation (even if you have to close your eyes)!   That last part is important. It helps build their confidence to try new things and increases their self esteem.

Below: The family pet rat, "Popsicle Hunter" was a faithful companion that attended all special occasions. Read more about "Popsicle Hunter" on page 109.

- Plan a day or week's worth of meals together. This opens up the lines of communication, provides quality time together, and teaches valuable skills.

- Create a menu from a grocery ad or a family member's favorite food. Create a shopping list from your menu.

- Using a grocery ad and a shopping list, add up the prices of three, four, and then five items. Try to do more.

- On a paper plate, use crayons, markers or colored pencils and draw your favorite foods.

- Cut out pictures from cardboard food boxes. Create a box of "food" to make pretend meals. Talk about nutritious and attractive meal planning. Use real plates and flatware.

- Have children read the directions to a recipe as you cook. Ask what comes next?

- Measure out the ingredients for a recipe together.

- Compare two different vegetables or fruits (or two different foods) that are the same color. For example: broccoli vs. green beans, banana vs. pear, carrot vs. orange.

- Create a new food. How would you market it? What kind of package would you put it in? What would the label look like?

- Make a list of your favorite vegetables or fruits.

- Invent a new sandwich.

- Using an ice shaver, make snow cones!

- *Shake-a-Pudding* - Instant pudding can be put in a jar and shaken for several minutes. Put into the refrigerator until set. Then enjoy.

- Have a shake-a -pudding party! Why not add music and shake away?

- Learn to make Jell-O®.

- Make lemonade with real lemons.

- Look at the skin inside an eggshell.

- Learn how to cook an egg. How many ways can eggs be cooked?

- Make a peanut butter and jelly sandwich. Have a picnic outside under a tree.

- Make your own edible play-dough. This recipe can be found on page 169. This is great for snack time.

- Use the pumpkin seeds from your Jack-o-Lantern to make roasted pumpkin seeds. Do this right in your kitchen oven.

- Cut up a real pumpkin and make a pumpkin pie.

- How many seeds are in the apple or orange you are eating?

- Become an anteater! You will need popcorn and a great sense of humor for this one. Place one piece of popcorn on your own shoulder. Very carefully (if you laugh you will blow the popcorn right off!) use your tongue to try to capture the popcorn. You will be rewarded for your efforts by getting to eat the popcorn. This makes for great photo opportunities!

- Pop and then string popcorn.

- Smell the spices in your kitchen. How are they alike? How are they different? Where do they come from? What do you use them for?

- Using the back of a placemat trace on the shapes of a place setting. This will assist young children in learning how to set the table as it becomes a matching game.

- Use place mats as a learning tool and source of table conversation. It also keeps little ones busy while waiting on dinner to be served. There are many available in the stores.

READ!

- Read, read, read! Read to your children, read with your children, have your children read to you, read as a family! Read chapter books as they get older. Discuss what you have read.

> Reading opens the doors for success, creativity, and imagination. It helps with critical thinking skills and is vital to survive in our society. Everything involves reading! Street signs, applications, instruction manuals, menus, recipes, the list goes on and on. Reading helps children do better in school.

One of my children did not like to read. So, we read together. I found magazines that he was interested in and he discovered he liked to read those. He could devour a technical instruction manual, but didn't like to read for fun. That's ok. He was still reading.

My other son loved books. He would read encyclopedias each night until he fell asleep. His bag would always be filled with books.

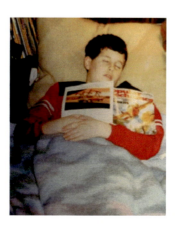

- Provide books for your children to read and explore. When you see that they are interested in a subject, find a book about it! Read it together. Let them investigate and learn.

    Author Story: I heard the excited yelling and the patter of little feet long before my four year old skidded to a stop in front of me holding a bird's nest. "Mom!, look what I found! Do we have a book about this?" My husband shook his head and smiled. Yes, we read books about every interest.

    When wires started dangling across the living room and my second grader installed a buzzer in the kitchen...so he "could call me when he needed me"...I decided I better come up with some books about electronics. Soon after, a door bell was installed to his room...all primitive systems, but worked nonetheless. To this day, that electronics book contains many page markers and the cover is tattered and worn.

- Before the addition of a new pet, read about it as a family to decide if everyone can meet the responsibilities it will bring to the family.

- Have children read directions, part of the newspaper, or comics out loud to you.

- Read a biography about an artist, musician, president or other famous person of interest.

- Read a poem.

- Memorize a poem and act out an after-dinner performance for the family.

- Tell stories about when you were growing up. Kids love to hear stories about when their parents and grandparents were children, in the "olden" days.

> Reading is the pathway to new knowledge. The more you read, the more you know how much more there is to learn!

BUILDING FAMILY UNITY

- Have a family fun night. Pick one day of the week to be your family bonding night. Play a game, do an activity, or go on a special outing on the particular day of the week your family has chosen.

    Our Family Night was on Friday. We would play miniature golf, visit Six Flags with our annual pass, play a board game or do some activity together.

    > Remember: Watching TV or going to a movie doesn't count! There is no interpersonal interaction, connection, sharing or communication that takes place while watching TV or a movie. Talking during the commercials doesn't count either.

- Create a monthly date with your child on their birth date. For example, if their birthday is September 9th, do something special each month on the ninth. Maybe have breakfast out with mom or dad or a special privilege for the day; examples: answering the phone, riding in the front seat of the car (if old enough), picking their favorite dinner, or playing their favorite game with the family.

- Count how many friends you have. What makes a good friend? What characteristics in a person do you think are important? (honesty, reliable, trustworthy, funny, humble, easy-going, etc.) How can you be a good friend?

- Celebrate the loss of a tooth!

DAILY QUESTION

- Create a daily question for family members each day. "What is today's question?" is a very fun activity to do with your children.

> Start chatting about just "stuff" with your children when they are very young. Talking about the little things when they are young, makes talking about the big things a lot easier when they get older.

- You and your children will have lots of fun with this activity. You will learn many things about each other. It won't be long before kids will be "hounding" you for the day's question. Everyone has a turn to answer the question and everyone else needs to respectfully listen to each person's answer. During each child's answer they must have your undivided attention for that moment. When you answer they must respectfully listen to you. Everyone involved in this is a winner as you learn to share, communicate, and respect other people's opinions and viewpoints.

- Below are some ideas to get you going. When you run out of questions, ask your children to help you generate more. Their creativity will be impressive and will tell you what is important to them.

    1. *What is your favorite?:* color, snack food, ice cream, candy, TV show, song, cookie, singer, sport, birthday cake, breakfast food, pie, sports team, subject to learn about (not a class in school), winter activity, summer activity, board game, card game, video game, pastime, cartoon, type of book, type of movie, vegetable, etc.

    2. Where is someplace you would like to visit?

    3. What is something you would NEVER do?

4. What is your favorite hobby? If you don't have a hobby, what is something that you are interested in learning about?

5. What is the vegetable you HATE the most?

6. How do you like your potatoes prepared, mashed, scalloped, au gratin, boiled, baked French fried?

7. What was your favorite Halloween costume?

8. What was your favorite Christmas present?

9. What was your most embarrassing moment?

10. What scares you the most?

11. What was a time you were really frightened?

12. What is a dream of yours?

13. If you could bring one person back to life to visit with, who would it be?

14. What is one thing you would like to do (a goal) in life?

15. What do you love to do the most?

16. What is something you would like to learn how to do?

17. Who would you like to meet in person some day?

Your ideas:

LEAVE A MESSAGE

- Leave a note on the bathroom mirror. Use soap, it will wash right off. This is a great idea just before cleaning day.

- Leave a kiss made with lipstick on the bathroom mirror, and a note telling your child they are loved and special.

- Post encouraging notes on the front door, in book bags, on the bathroom mirror, on the front of the refrigerator, pantry door, inside the cover of a book they are reading or in a textbook, on their pillow, inside their shoe (they will find it when putting them on), in a jacket, shirt or pant pockets or anyplace else you can think of where your child will find the note.

- Leave a message with marker on the cereal box or a note in the box as the child pours out their cereal.

- Post-It® notes work great to leave notes in creative places. *The possibilities are endless. Be creative!*

- Use picture messages for children who can not read yet

THE TIES THAT BIND US...
FOR WHEN YOU CANNOT BE TOGETHER

- Video record a special adult (parent, grandparent, relative, etc.) reading your children's favorite stories. This is a comfort for a child who must be separated from an adult they love or if they want to be read to when the adult in charge is in the middle of something and can't stop to read. Children can follow along with the book.

- Apply bright lipstick and then kiss a cardboard/construction paper heart. Write on it, "A good night kiss from mom or dad." On the other side glue a picture of the person the kiss is from.

- Lipstick is also good for kissing mirrors along with a message written with a bar of soap. (don't worry, it washes off on cleaning day). This is a great way to leave a reminder for children too. Don't forget to leave the X & O (hugs and kisses) at the end.

- Seal a card with a "kiss" along with a special message inside the card. Leave it in a spot they will find.

PUZZLES

Puzzles can be made in just a few seconds or you can get a bit more creative making them last for longer than one play time.

- Food box puzzle

Cereal boxes tend to be colorful, but many other food boxes can make delightful puzzles also. The front or back can be cut into the age appropriate number of pieces to entertain children.

Remember: Younger children need fewer pieces than older children. Start with two to three pieces for your two and three year old children and work up to many pieces for the eight to twelve year old child.

Puzzles are great to do while waiting for dinner. Empty the food box and hand it over to the older child to create their own puzzle, or quickly cut the cardboard apart for your younger child.

Puzzles can be randomly cut into pieces or you can use cookie cutters to cut shapes out of the cardboard making an inlay puzzle.

A shape game can be made by making a spinner with the corresponding shapes used in the puzzle. The child spins, identifies the shape, then looks for that piece and inserts it into the puzzle.

An inlaid puzzle can be made by gluing a solid piece of cardboard (the other side of the box) to the back of the puzzle. The puzzle pieces will not fall through the puzzle with this method.

- Greeting card puzzle

This type of puzzle is easy to make. Cut an old greeting card into a variety of shaped pieces. You can use a cookie cutter to hide a shape(s) within the puzzle to make it more fun. If you have two of the same card you can glue or tape a complete picture on the front of the envelope. Place the cut up pieces inside the envelope and label how many pieces are in that puzzle.

- Calendar puzzle

Calendars have great photos that can be used after the end of the year. Cut them out and glue them onto cardboard for stability. Then cut out the pieces that you desire. Place the pieces in a labeled bag or envelope. The label should tell what is in the picture and how many pieces are in the puzzle.

- Photo puzzle

Any photograph can be cut apart using the same methods described before to create a personalized puzzle. For a sturdier puzzle, glue to a piece of thin cardboard before cutting out the shapes. A message can be written with a permanent fine tipped marker on the photo before cutting it apart.

This type of puzzle is fun to send as a greeting card for children who are celebrating a birthday or are sick. This is an especially nice idea for a relative or grandparent. Once the child puts the puzzle together, they see their loved one.

- Meat tray inlay puzzle

This type of puzzle is successful for much younger children. Using cookie cutters, cut simple shapes out of a clean Styrofoam® meat tray. You can choose one shape to start with. Another idea is to have a progression of sizes of the same shape (small, medium, large). Use several shapes for a more advanced puzzle.

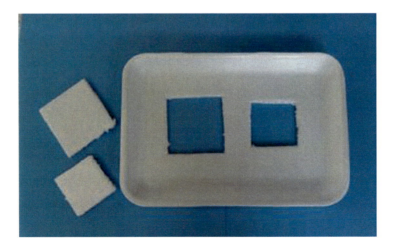

Miraculous Magical Moments in Minutes 51

- Fill a shape puzzle

Provide your child with the resulting shape and a bag of puzzle pieces. They need to fill in the shape to put their puzzle together.

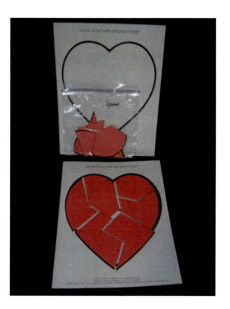

- Cracked shape puzzle

These puzzles work great for hearts, eggs, and anything else you can think of. Children must find the two pieces that go together. This is great to develop visual discrimination. Cookie cutters can be used to create these puzzles.

PUZZLE MAKING TIPS

It is always helpful to see the picture that you are putting together. So, use two identical cards. Cut one apart for the puzzle. Glue or tape the whole card onto the front of the envelope or storage container for the pieces.

Store puzzles in an envelope or labeled plastic sealed bag that tells what the picture is and how many pieces are inside.

Children can help make puzzles as soon as they are old enough to use scissors.

> Remember: Younger children need fewer pieces than older children. Make puzzles with 2-3 pieces for the smaller child and progress to more complex puzzles as children become more skilled.

GUESSING GAMES

- Who's there? "Peek-a-Boo" folders

Glue a large picture of a familiar character inside a file folder. This can be a picture from a magazine, from the computer, or a photograph. A photo of a face, the child or a family member, or even the family pet would be fun to put inside.

On the cover, cut out little doors in different places. You can make one door in the middle or several smaller doors. Children can take turns opening the doors revealing parts of the picture underneath, guessing what is inside.

This develops vocabulary and increases understanding of how the sum of parts equals a whole.

- Micro-view window

Find a piece of cardstock, colored paper or construction paper. Cut out shapes or little "windows" in the center of the paper. Food box fronts that have plastic windows also work well. Take a look at magazine pictures, photos, flowers, things around the house or yard. What do you see? If only looking at a small part of a picture, can you tell what the whole object is? Draw what you see? Georgia Totto O'Keeffe (November 15, 1887 – March 6, 1986) was an American artist who used this technique. Why not look up some of her paintings or read about her career as an artist.

- Who am I?

Paste a large picture of an animal inside an old file folder. Cut off enough of the front of the folder to just let the ears of the animal show. Children guess what animal has those ears. When they open the folder, they can see the whole animal.

- Where's my feet?

Use pictures of animals. Cut the picture apart separating the animal body from the feet. If desired, laminate the pictures before you cut them out for greater longevity of the game. Children match the feet to the correct animal. After playing this game is a great time to investigate and research about the animals in the game. Where do they live? What do they eat? Where do they sleep? Etc.

MATCHING GAMES

> Where's the pair? Matching games build observation and classification skills through left–right association (for the socks and mittens), size relationship, and color differentiation.

- **Match real socks**

  When doing laundry make a game out of matching the socks. This will make the weekly chore go quickly.

- **Paper pairs**

  You can match anything! Hearts, Easter eggs, flowers, animals, socks, mittens, etc.

  Use cookie cutters or stencils to make two matching shapes from old wallpaper books, cardstock, heavy wrapping paper or construction paper.

- Fabric squares

    Make a matching game that involves the sense of touch by using a variety of textures, colors, and patterns.

- Picture Lotto

    Objective: To find the pictures that match and put into pairs. This game increases memory and observation skills.

    Directions: Older players can place all the cards face down in a pile. Take turns trying to find a pair. If successful, the player gets another turn. If not, place the cards face down in the pile. Then the other player gets a turn. Younger children select a picture, then find the matching picture to make it a pair.

    Use the computer, magazines, photos, etc. to find pictures. Use topics that interest your child and family. If desired, laminate the pages with clear contact paper, then cut out the pairs. Store in a labeled envelope or sealed plastic bag.

    Examples:

    - Random photos of interest

- Mothers and their babies.

Use animals or people. If using people you could use a picture of mom and children that are in your family or that your child actually knows.

- Animals and their footprints

- Seeds and the plants they produce.

- Seasons

Design two pictures for each season and headings that list each season. You decide what picture comes to mind when you think of each season. For example: Spring=baby birds and an umbrella; Summer=beach ball and a full sun; Fall=pumpkin and Fall leaves; Winter=snowman and a snowflake.

Children match up the pairs and decide which season it is.

- Posters

    Any poster that shows a variety of items can become quick matching games. For example, a poster of state or country flags, different types of trees, flowers, fish, animals etc.

    Buy two posters and have them both laminated. Leave one whole and cut the other one into matching pieces. It then becomes a matching game.

LACE-UP CARDS

- Also called sewing cards. This activity develops fine motor skills.

    Greeting cards, old calendar pictures glued onto cardboard, food box fronts, etc., can be used to make a lace-up card.

    Use a hole punch to make holes around the outside edge.

    Take a shoelace or yarn to lace up the picture.

    If using yarn or cording, wrap masking or packing tape around the ends to make it stiff. Then it can be easily laced through the holes.

PUPPETS
Puppets can be made with a variety of materials

- Sock puppet

    The single sock with no mate that appears on laundry day can become a source of hours of entertainment.

    Decorate the sock with buttons, fabric scraps, felt, sequins, markers, yarn, etc.

    Insert your hand through the top of the sock and a puppet appears.

- Sock story books

    After you have created the puppets, go to the next level by writing and illustrating a story book about the puppet's life. Act out the story for any willing audience!

     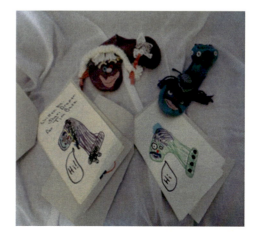

- Paper sack puppet

    Use a folded paper lunch bag. Insert your hand through the top of the bag. Your fingers slip into the fold and waving action creates the puppet's mouth. Decorate as you wish.

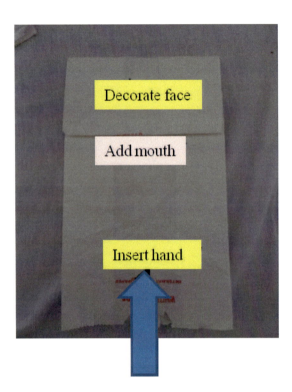

Cut out eyes, nose and mouth pictures from magazines or faces from computer clip art. Glue them on the sack to make your puppet face.

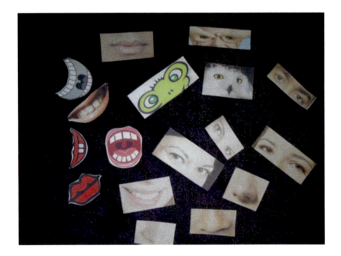
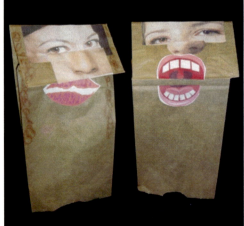

Miraculous Magical Moments in Minutes 63

- Envelope puppet

    Envelopes convert easily into a puppet. First fold in the flap or take it off. Place your thumb and middle finger in each of the bottom corners, squeeze, folding the envelope in half. You are ready to decorate with markers, crayons, colored pencils, felt, yarn, stickers or anything else you can think of. Then it is time to play!

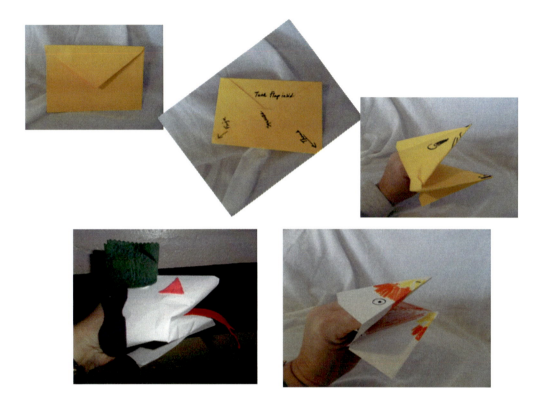

- Fist puppet

    Make a loose fist with your thumb tucked in. The space on the side of your fist, between your thumb and finger, becomes the mouth. Draw lips here. Draw eyes on the knuckle of your index finger.

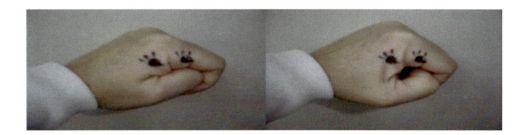

- Finger puppets

    Draw faces on your finger(s) and you are ready for a puppet show. In the picture below, meet my "family": Spot the dog (thumb) Momma, Poppa, Brother and Sister. You can make them any way you want.

    This type of puppet is a life saver when waiting anywhere with fidgety children. All you need is a pen and you can create instant fun.

- Glove puppets

    Many times children's winter gloves are cute animals or characters. These make good puppets all year long.

    Sometimes you can find children's washcloth gloves at stores. These make great puppets too.

    A pair of jersey work gloves or the knit stretch gloves can be made into puppets. Draw faces on each finger like you did for the finger puppets. The nice thing about glove puppets is that you can also decorate them with yarn hair, wiggle eyes, felt clothes, ribbon etc. This is a fun way to act out a favorite story. Decorate a finger for each character in the story, then take turns acting out the story line.

- Shadow puppets—see page 96.

- Face puppets—see page 155.

- Balloon puppet

    Blow up a balloon and draw a face on it. Do not tie the balloon closed. Deflate and keep in your pocket. Then, pull out your "balloon buddy" whenever you need an attention getter. This is especially fun and effective for transition between activities for younger children. Older children will enjoy making their own balloon cast of characters.

    I used to sing a little tune, when the balloon I called "Betty" wanted my four year old preschool class to do something. The words were:

    "Betty Balloon, Betty Balloon,
     Betty Balloon says to…. (action desired)."
    Action examples: sit right down, come to me, pick up the toys, etc.

    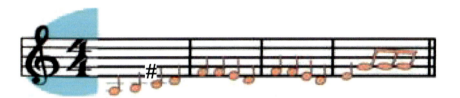

    You can make up any tune, words, and name for your balloon.

- Puppet tips

    Home made puppets are great for times when you are waiting. Put on a funny voice, make silly expressions and you can entertain children for hours. Or they can entertain themselves or you.

    Create books about your puppets. What is going on in their lives, where do they live, what do they like and dislike. This is a great way to "see" into your child's thoughts as they create their puppet's storybook.

    Don't forget to let children put on puppet shows. Use a cardboard box, the back of a couch, a card table covered with a blanket or anything else you can dream up to perform the function of a puppet stage. It will provide hours of entertainment for young and old alike. Make sure there is a healthy round of applause after the performance. And, don't forget to take pictures!

MUSIC

- Compose a song.

    Make up a song. Create happy, sad, fast or slow songs. Sing about how your day is going, about the trees or flowers, about your pet, or big or little sister/brother. You can make up a song about anything.

    Do you have a favorite melody? Create your own words to familiar songs.

    Compose songs to help you memorize a phone number, address, spelling words, etc.

    Make up songs to give directions: clean up, bedtime, brushing your teeth, etc. When directions and instructions are put to music, kids perk up, smile and "hop" right to the task.

- Put on a musical show for the family.

- Name that tune.

    One person hums a tune. The other person guesses what song it is. Try humming just the first line. Can you still guess the song?

- Sing a nursery rhyme. Don't know the tune? Make one up!

- Sing the alphabet song.

- Sing a song together.

- Practice whistling.

- Dance

    Did your favorite song just come on the radio? Grab a child and enjoy a dance. Make up the steps or learn how to waltz, polka, swing and other popular fun dances.

- Learn how to play an instrument.

- Marching band/concert

    If you do not know how to play an instrument, don't let that stop you! "Play" a concert or have a marching band performance.

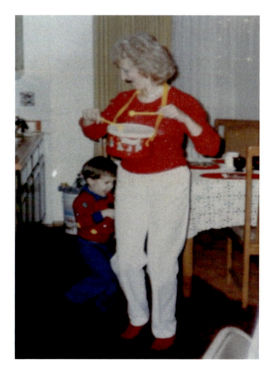

HAND AND FOOT FUN

- File folder stencil

    Trace around a child's hand/foot on the front of a manila file folder. Have the child sign and date the image. With a matte knife (adults only here) cut out the print creating a stencil. Then children can slip any color sheet of paper they want into the file and trace their hand/foot shape. The file folder keeps the paper from slipping which causes frustration for children. This activity also provides great memorabilia for parents too.

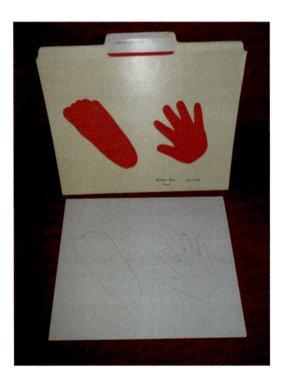

- Draw around your hands and feet.

    Trace around the child's hand on a piece of paper, then with crayons, markers or colored pencils create a miniature world inside.

- Handprint creations

    A traditional creation is the hand print turkey.

    Handprints can be combined around a circle to make a wreath. Fingerprints can be added for berries. This creation can be made on paper, a decoration on the front of a shirt or on a fabric banner to hang on the wall.

A foot print and hands can be transformed into an angel, using a pipe cleaner or garland for a halo.

A foot shape can become the body of a reindeer and the hands become the antlers.

The possibilities are endless… let your imagination go!

MIRROR, MIRROR ON THE WALL...

Looking in mirrors establishes identity and a sense of self.
Babies love to look at themselves in the mirror!

- Look in the mirror.

    Make silly faces.

    Compare eye and hair color.

    Open wide and count your teeth.

- Empty powder compacts

    It is fun for children to look in the mirrors found inside. Decorate with stickers

- Draw yourself!

    Look in the mirror and draw yourself.

- Mirror images

    Stand facing a partner. You can play music if you want to. Start out slowly, gradually lifting one arm and then the other. Move your legs or feet. See if your partner can copy you. Watch in a mirror to see if you are moving at the same time. Switch roles and try again.

DRESS UP – DRAMATIC ROLE PLAYING

Dramatic play fosters imagination and creativity while simultaneously encouraging thinking, reasoning, language, and social development. Imagination enables children to become in play what they cannot yet be in real life. Through dramatic play children can act out and work through their fears, worries and anxieties. For example, going to the doctor. By "play acting" this situation children can play the role of being in control. This results in their fears being reduced.

Dramatic play utilizes materials to represent a variety of situations or experiences. Be creative and have fun. If you have trouble pulling together ideas for role playing, consult the greatest creative experts…. your children!

Below are some ideas. You do not have to have all the materials for this type of play. Start with a few items and add as you and your child think of more ideas.

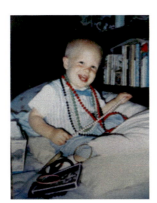

- Family life

    Dolls and accessories, dishes, pots and pans, utensils, table cloth and child size table, play money, empty toiletry and cleaning containers, telephones, small note pads, pencils, stationary, envelopes. (Save return envelopes from junk mail. Children love to write messages and seal the envelopes to "mail.")

    Dress-up clothes, hats, jackets, blouses, shirts, gloves, shoes, ties, etc. These items can be old items or articles temporarily borrowed from your closet. What a treat to wear something "real!"

- Birthday party

    Party hats, balloons and a banner, a cake (cookie, cupcake or small box decorated).

    Presents (empty boxes wrapped in decorative paper or the comic papers). Lids of boxes can be wrapped or covered in pretty contact paper with the addition of a bow to be used as fake presents. Small toys or jewelry can be put inside the boxes for pretend presents.

- Tea party

    Set of cups and saucers, plastic pitcher, napkins, trays, vase of silk flowers, tablecloth, plastic silverware, pretend food (cardboard, plastic, paper, empty grocery containers) or real food (oyster crackers for tea cakes, small muffins or cupcakes, tiny cookies).

- Baby nursery

    Baby dolls, sink (dish pan or baking pan), small bar of soap (hotel samples), towel and wash cloth, baby blankets, baby clothes, bibs, diaper bags (old real ones, or an old purse), baby bottles, small bowl and spoon, bed (shoe box, plastic storage bin), diapers, toiletries (wet wipes, empty baby lotion and powder containers), rocking chair, baby food (empty containers from real food or small cereal boxes or juice boxes).

- Doctor/Nurse

    White lab coat, surgical gown, doctor's kit or bag, stethoscope, bandages, rubber gloves, pencil, flashlight, telephone, clipboard.

- Cleaning

    Broom and dustpan (child size), bucket, sponges, rubber gloves, spray bottle, paper towels.

- Laundry

    Dish pan, clothes line, clothes pins, doll clothes, clothes basket, child size ironing board and iron (a table and a wooden block can be used).

- Circus

    Crazy hats, costumes, and a ruffled collar for clowns, face paint, tickets, huge balls, balloons, a 2x4 for a tight rope or balance beam, stuffed animals, large hoop, paper streamers to make a tent, mirror, popcorn, soft drinks.

- Zoo

    Boxes or laundry baskets (turned upside down for cages), stuffed or plastic animals, wagon/truck.

- Farm/Ranch

    Child size gardening tools, green rug for a field or yard, stuffed or plastic animals, cowboy/farmer hats, barn (can use a cardboard box), seeds, stick horse, red bandana, farm vehicles.

- Beach

    Towels, beach umbrella, hats, sunglasses, a sand box (indoor or outside), water play (indoors or outside) and water toys, radio, sea shells, beach balls.

- Fish pond

    Blue rug/towel or sheet, boats (boxes or laundry baskets to sit in), fishing poles (sticks with yarn or string tied on one end and a paper clip "hook" attached), paper or toy fish, nets, worms (gummy worms, rubber bands or Styrofoam® packing peanuts).

- Camp site

    Tent (blanket over chairs/table or real tent), flashlight, campfire (cardboard tubes or sticks), sleeping bag, back pack, snacks (granola bars, beef jerky), compass, maps, ice chest, cooking utensils.

- Restaurant

    Small table and table cloth, napkins, dishes, vase with silk flowers, old menus from real restaurants (or make your own), order pads and pencils, music, play money and cash register (can be made with a flat box that opens up with a hinged lid, egg cartons work well also), trays, placemats, play food (plastic, paper, grocery ads, food boxes or pictures cut out of magazines), chef or restaurant hats.

- Fast food

    Food containers, paper sacks, glasses with lids, and napkins from your favorite fast food restaurant.

- Library

    Desk, shelves, books, index cards, rubber stamps and ink pad, cozy place to read (bean bag chair), pencils, return slot or receptacle (cardboard box with a slot cut into the side or a large canvas bag).

- Grocery store

    Empty food cartons and cans with the labels still on (cut the bottoms out of cans when cooking, so the cans can be used in role playing. Be sure there are no sharp edges.), baskets/bags, coupons, grocery store ads, cash register, play money.

- Garden and flower store/Gardener

    Small silk flowers/plants, plastic or paper fruits and vegetables, basket to gather flowers and vegetables, watering can, gardening gloves, seeds, flower pots (yogurt or margarine containers), gardening tools (child size).

- Pet store/Veterinarian's office

    Doctor's props, empty fish tank/bird cage, collars, leashes, food dishes, cages (cardboard box or upside down laundry basket), stuffed or plastic animals, books on animals.

- Airport

    Badges, taped shape of an airplane on the floor, chairs in a row, belts for seat belts, steering wheel, travel items (brochures, maps, postcards, books about other places), suit cases with luggage tags, dinner trays.

    A large cardboard box flattened out can be drawn on with marker to make an airport. Use toy airplanes to fly in and out of the airport.

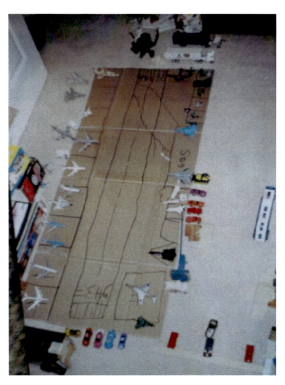

- Post Office

    Letters, postcards, square stickers for stamps, stationary, envelopes (save return envelopes from junk mail). A mail box can be made from a cardboard box.

Miraculous Magical Moments in Minutes

- Other role playing kit ideas

    Shoe store, hardware store, wedding/bridal shop, travel agency, train station, office, beauty salon/barber, firefighter, police officer, plumber, theater, movie theater, school, bank, radio station, dentist, rodeo, science lab, band, feed store, etc.

- Dramatic role playing tips

    - Kit storage

    Dramatic play props can be kept in Rubbermaid® containers, shoeboxes, or cardboard boxes. Clearly label the outside of each dramatic play prop box.

    - Prop sources

    Dramatic play props can be found in closets, storerooms, attics, garages and many places in your community. Keep your eyes open and listen to your children for ideas.

> Your life experiences, hobbies, occupations and situations related to your family can be an inspiration for new ideas. The sky is the limit. Let your imagination soar! Again, let your children be your guide.

CARPET AND YARN

- Carpet drawings

    Using yarn or string, "draw" pictures on carpeting, carpet rectangles, rugs, towels or blankets. Dangle the string onto the surface to form a design. If you don't like what you made, simply pull the string to make changes or start over. Use several different colors of yarn to make your design multi-colored.

- Ride a magic carpet

    Use a towel, blanket, or carpet rectangle and then "climb" on your magic carpet sitting in the middle. Close your eyes and away you go! Imagine the carpet rising into the sky. Look below. What do you see? Where are you going?

    Maybe you would like to use it to see all the special things around you that are missed in a hurried life.

NEWSPAPER FUN

- Letter search

    Want some practice at letters? Following specific directions? Try this letter search. It can be easily modified for different age groups. You will need an old magazine or newspaper and some colored pencils or markers. Letter recognition can be practiced by circling every letter found that starts with the letter in your first or last name. Maybe look for all the letters in your name and underline them. Have children underline one letter you designate in one color, circle another designated letter in a different color, and put a square in yet another color for a different designated letter. Older children can look for vowels (a,e,i,o,u), or pairs of letters that make sounds like "th," "br," or prefixes (pre, dis, pro) and suffixes (ed, ing, es). Older children may also like to have races, seeing how many designated letters they can find in a certain amount of time, or in one article.

- Initial search

    Circle all the words that start with the first letter in your name. Now look for the first letter in your last name or your middle initial.

- Funny pictures

    Draw beards, mustaches and funny designs on the pictures in the newspaper.

- Newspaper fashion show

    You will need tape, scissors, a stapler and lots of imagination as you design complete outfits, purses, shoes, hats, jewelry, coats…all out of newspaper! Designate an announcer and model your creations.

- Newspaper hat or boat—see page 173.

EXPLORATION

> By allowing children to engage in exploration you are fostering their scientific thinking skills. Exploration refines the ability to pay attention to specific details, enables them to predict, investigate, analyze, reason and problem solve resulting in development of new concepts and construction of their own ideas.

- How is it put together? What makes it work?

    Use a screwdriver and pliers to take apart a broken clock, radio, watch, etc. How does it work? What is inside? Putting it back together is not important for this type of play. The adventure of the journey is the important fact.

- Flashlight challenge

    Take apart a flashlight and put it back together! Does it work?

    Author story: My youngest son was always taking things apart! With and without permission! So, I finally wised up. Every time we went to a garage sale or re-sale shop he was given fifty cents to a dollar to spend on what he wished. He always bought something he could explore. This resulted in boxes of parts in his "work room" in the basement. From those supplies he created many fun, surprising things.

CONSTRUCTION

> Construction materials and toys foster creativity and imagination. It teaches principles of design and engineering. *It is important to remember play is the work and occupation of children. It is how they learn.*

- Familiar construction toys provide a variety of open-ended play materials.

    Examples: Lego's, Tinker Toys, Erector Sets, Lincoln Logs

- Marshmallows and toothpicks

    Using toothpicks and marshmallows, become an architect and make a structure, build a house or sky scraper. Eat your creation, after a photo shoot, of course! Toothpicks need to be used carefully and thrown away after use.

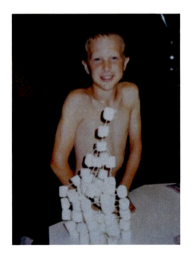

- Q-Tips® and glue

    These materials make great structures and is practice in your architectural skills.

- Make a teepee or a megaphone out of a circle of paper. Decorate it.

- Make a paper airplane.

    Create different designs. Which one flies the straightest? Which one flies the farthest? Why?

- Build a tent!

    Make a tent with blankets and if necessary, a piece of rope. Good places: between two trees, over clothes lines, under the picnic table, or a card table, between several kitchen chairs or furniture, under the kitchen table.

- The real thing!

    Build something together with real tools.

    Author story: When my son was five years old he wanted tools for Christmas. He made it very plain that he didn't want the "fake" plastic tools. He wanted the real thing! He was very interested in how to use the tools. Of course, when the interest is high, that is the time to teach! So, he got a bright red, real tool box with a few basic real tools inside. Many sessions were spent in the garage with his father learning the principles of quality construction and the proper use of tools. That son became my handy-man. He could fix just about anything!

- Practice, practice, practice!

    Learning fine motor skills, and the correct way to use a tool, is important.

    Use a large piece of Styrofoam®, (like the type that is used in packing a box), old golf tees, a small wooden hammer and goggles. Practice hammer skills by hammering the golf tees into the Styrofoam®.

    Children should wear goggles for this activity.

LONG TIME FAVORITES

- Drop the clothespin in a bottle.

    If you don't have any clothespins, play a modified version of this long time favorite. Use an unsharpened pencil and an empty food container or bottle. The older the child, the smaller the opening. The younger the child the larger the opening should be. Can you drop a pencil from waist high into a soda bottle?

Becky as a child (on the left)

- Hang a tire swing.

- Pin the tail on the donkey.

    When it is your turn, you must be blind folded. Someone spins you around a few times and aims you in the right direction. Try to get the missing piece onto the picture in the correct location.

    We have played many versions of this game throughout the years. It doesn't have to be a donkey. It can be almost any picture. Be creative.

    Ideas:

    Stick the nose on your favorite cartoon character, animal or a clown.

    Put the spots on a leopard. Use round colored stickers like they use for garage sale pricing. Sketch an animal on a large piece of cardboard and stand or tape it to something to make it stand up.

- Learn how to operate a yo-yo and do tricks.

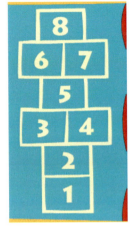

- Play Hop-Scotch.

   Small rocks, a link of broken chain or a bean bag can be used to take turns throwing onto a number. Where it lands, is where you stop hopping. Hop on one foot for the single numbers, both feet down on the numbers side by side. If your non-hopping foot comes down on the single numbers, it is the next person's turn. If you get really good, hop to the end and back!

   The hop scotch pattern can be drawn with chalk on the sidewalk or basement floor. Masking tape can be used in these spots also. You can even make an indoor game of hop scotch on a carpet or tile floor. Make sure you remove the tape immediately after the game to prevent sticky residue. If using masking tape inside, the best tape is the blue painters tape that comes off easily.

- Practice snapping your fingers.

- Play catch.

   Football, Baseball, Frisbee, Nerf ball. Even a foil, paper sack, or sock ball.

- Blow bubbles—see page 146, and recipe on page 170.

- Jump rope—see page 136.

- Learn to play jacks.

- Learn to play marbles.

> If you have not played these games before, directions for jacks, marbles and tic-tac-toe can be found online.

- Play tic-tac-toe. Play the best of two games out of three.

- Blow up a paper bag and then POP it!

- Sing or say a Mother Goose nursery rhyme.

    Examples: Jack and Jill, Do you Know the Muffin Man?, Little Miss Muffet, Mary Had a Little Lamb, Old Mother Hubbard, The Cat and the Fiddle, Twinkle, Twinkle Little Star, Humpty Dumpty, Hickory Dickory Dock, Baa Baa Black Sheep, Little Jack Horner, etc.

    Can you think of actions or activities to fit the theme of your favorite nursery rhyme?

    Author story: A favorite nursery rhyme at our house was "Do you know the Muffin Man?". Many performances were given with this rhyme while standing on a stuffed chair or in the car driving someplace. We played "muffin man" with play dough and muffin tins. We pretended to sell and eat them. This rhyme generated many play ideas.

- Make old fashioned Valentines or cards.

    Use doilies (found at discount stores), ribbons, lace, construction paper, stickers, markers and crayons to create that perfect card for someone special.

- Go for a walk and DON'T step on any cracks.

    This is really fun on a sidewalk that is broken into many pieces. When I was in grade school the saying went, "don't step on a crack or you will break your mother's back!".

- Play hide and seek.

- Play hide the thimble.

    This was a favorite many decades ago. Many people don't have thimbles now. Why not take the same idea and hide some other small object? Examples: matchbox car, action figure, comb, pencil, etc.

- Egg Hunt

    Use plastic eggs, so if one is not found, it won't spoil. Give everyone their own sack or basket. Take turns hiding and finding the eggs. You can hide other things too. How about cotton balls?

- Play "I see, I see" or "I Spy."

    Say, "I Spy" or "I see, I see, something ____." The other player(s) ask questions to try to guess what is being spied. The person "spying" can only answer yes or no. You may want to say "warmer" or "colder" if the person is close to or far away from the chosen object. When it has been correctly guessed, it is the other person's turn.

- Play "20 Questions".

    Directions: Pick a person to start. That person must think of an object. To make the game easier, decide before hand if it is an animal, vegetable or mineral. If not pre-determined, this should be your first question to determine the classification. Another player asks a question that can only be answered yes or no. The person thinking of the object can only respond with a simple yes or no. No extra clues should be given! Players are allowed to ask 20 different questions. After hearing the answer, the person asking the question may try to guess the object. If the guess is correct, the person who guessed correctly gets to think of a new object. If the object is not revealed within 20 questions, the object must be revealed and a new object is picked.

    > "I Spy " and "20 Questions" are great games to occupy children while you are waiting, on a rainy day, long car ride, doctor's office wait, grocery line wait, etc. These games use listening, comprehension, & deductive listening skills.

- Learn to braid

    You can use yarn, string, shoe laces, cording etc. to learn to braid. One end needs to be secured. This can be done by someone holding one end. You can also hammer a nail into a small 1x4 board and tie one end of the cords to the nail to secure them. A food box container front also works well for a securing board. Punch a hole in one end and tie the cords through the hole. Make sure to use three different colors as you begin to learn. Alternate the right and left cord over the middle cord until your braid is as long as you want.

- Learn to play a card game!

    Old Maid, Go Fish, Rummy,
    Spoons (four of a kind), Concentration

- Invent your own card or board game.

- Play a board game with the whole family! Grandparents too!

- Learn to play checkers.

- Have a checker tournament.

BODY CHALLENGES

- Do jumping jacks or sit ups.

- How many somersaults can you do?

- Stand on your head.

    Can you stand on your head? How long can you hold it?

    Author story: My dad could still stand on his head when I left home for college. We used to have contests…he always beat me. Over the years my sons joined in on the competition. Here are some photos to help you get started.

- Keep your balance!

    Stand with your heels against the wall. Place an object at your feet. Can you pick it up without moving your feet? Bet you can't, but it will be worth the laughs!

- Skip

    Skip to the mailbox from the backdoor. How long does it take. Is it shorter or faster than walking or running?

- Sports

    Decide as a family a new sport to do together (fishing, dancing, roller skating, skate boarding, swimming, bicycle riding, etc.)

- Hop on one foot.

    Hop on one foot and then the other. How many times can you hop on each foot?

- Circles and waves

    Make circles and waves with your hands and feet. Can you do it at the same time? Can you go different directions at the same time?

- Hang a spoon from your nose.

    Caution: laughing may get out of hand!

    Metal spoons tend to work best, but plastic spoons can be used.

- Practice making bows.

    Put a bow on the family pet, if they will allow it. Put bows on all the stuffed animals and in the hair of all the dolls. Use different colors and widths of ribbon.

- Learn to tie a shoe.

    Trace around your shoe on cardboard or use an empty food container box (like cereal). Punch two rows of four holes each. Tie together two different colored shoe laces, cording, or heavy yarn and use them as laces. The two colors help you see better how to make the bow. Adults can say, "now take the white lace and go over," etc.

    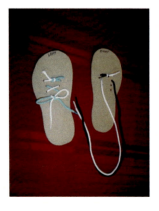

- Jumping bean

    This can be done anywhere inside or outside. You will need a tape measure and some spring in your jump. Jump as far as you can from one spot to another. Measure the distance. Have contests with each other, between siblings, friends or children against adults. Try to beat your record. Chart your progress to add more math skill to the fun.

- Walk a tight rope.

    Pretend you are walking on a tight rope. Use yarn, a tape measure, masking tape or a 2x4 piece of wood on the floor as your pretend rope.

- Curl your tongue.

    Can you curl your tongue? Do both sides go up or just one? This activity is also susceptible to giggling fits.

- Count your teeth.

    How many teeth do you have on the top? Bottom? All together?

- Take your pulse.

    Your pulse can be found on the inside of your wrist or on the side of your neck. Press two fingers to one of these spots. Do not use your thumbs! Count each time you feel a beat, timing your pulse for 15 seconds. Take this number and multiply it by four.

    Now run in place and take your pulse again. What happened to your heart rate? Younger children will learn where their heart is and the concept that more work causes our heart to pump harder.

- Silly string

    Have a silly string challenge. Wear old clothes, as sometimes the dyes in the silly string can stain fabric. This is best done outdoors or on a cement floor.

- Catch

    Of course, we have already mentioned the traditional ways to play catch. But, why not try playing catch with milk carton "mitts" and sock balls. Cut the ends off of two clean, empty plastic milk cartons. The size (gallon or quart) will determine how much of a challenge you want. The carton handle will be your hand grip. Then roll up an old clean sock to toss back and forth. You can use your carton to throw or to catch the ball.

    Cartons can be decorated to look like fish or monsters catching "food."

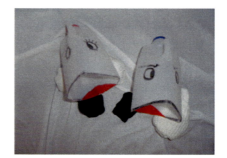

- Ball toss/Score a point

    Empty tin cans (with smooth edges) can be used individually or bound together with rubber bands, string or yarn. Write points on each can. Score points by tossing a small ball, a bean bag, a foil ball or rolled up sock into the cans.

- Indoor "golf"

    Use a tin can (with smooth edges) a yard stick or ruler and a ball of some type. Balls can be rolled up socks or foil balls. Create a "putting" range on any smooth surface.

- Create a silly face.

    Have a family contest to see who can make the silliest face.

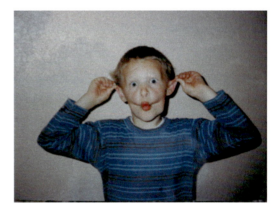

- Learn to thread a needle.

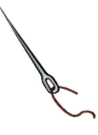

- Learn to sew on a button.

- Sew a garment.

    Using scrap fabric or felt, create a shirt or dress for a doll.

BALLOONS

- Balloon fun

    Of course we know we can bounce them, stomp them, sit on them and play volley ball with them, but here are a few more things to do with balloons.

- Message balloons

    Write a message on a piece of paper. Ideas: Hug someone you like, sing a song, pat your head, hop on one foot, etc. Fold this message and insert it into a balloon. Decorate your balloon with a marker before you blow it up. After a game of Balloon Toss (keeping the balloon in the air as long as possible before it touches the floor), pop your balloon and do whatever the message inside tells you to do. One or all of these should produce lots of laughter!

- Static electric balloons

    Can you make a balloon stick to your hair or a wall? Can you get it to pick up thread or some other lightweight object? You can build a negative electrical charge by rubbing an inflated balloon on someone's hair. Tiny particles (electrons) move from the hair to the balloon. The balloon will now stick to various things. How many things can you find that are uncharged that you can make it stick to?

- Singing balloons

    Who has not made funny noises with a deflating balloon's "neck?" Inflate a balloon but do not tie it. Stretch its neck as the air escapes. You can make singing and silly noises.

- Critters and shapes

    Twist and turn long skinny balloons to make animals and shapes.

- Balloon puppet —see page 65.

- Floating/flying experiments

    At our house, many boats and planes were created with the use of a balloon. Not all of the experiments worked, but it was fun and a good learning experience.

    Give your older kids some balloons, tape and spare "parts" from their exploration play and let them create. Being the photo journalist for these experiences and encourager will be some of your favorite memories.

FLASHLIGHT FUN

- Flashlight flashcards

    Take a deck of flashcards, on any subject, (you can even make your own with note cards or card stock) and throw them on the floor. Make sure all are facing up. Then using a flashlight, shine the light on a card. Kids love to be the spotlight! The card with the spotlight becomes the challenge for the child to solve. Ex. 9+1 = and the child says 10! If the child is correct, the card is picked up. If the child is incorrect, it stays on the floor. When all the cards have been answered correctly the game is done.

- Dancing light beams

    While lying down in a darkened room, turn on your flashlight and make it "dance" around the ceiling. This is great fun with two or even three people.

- Make shadows

    Put your hand in front of a flashlight beam to make shadows on the wall or ceiling. A fist with two fingers held up straight can be a hopping bunny. Movement of your thumb snapped up to your fingers becomes a crocodile. What other animals can you make?

    Hold up different objects and guess what the object is. Move the object closer to the light and then farther away from the light to make the object bigger and smaller. How does the distance from the light change the shape of the shadow?

- Have a shadow puppet show!

    Animals or paper shapes (made out of cardboard or construction paper) glued to popsicle sticks held in front of a flashlight beam makes shadows on the wall. Make up a story as you go along.

FISHING POND
for fun or learning facts

Materials needed:

- A blue towel, rug or sheet — it becomes your pond.
- Fishing poles — use a stick from the yard or a short dowel rod.
- Fishing line and "hook" — cut a piece of string or yarn and tie it to the end of the stick. On the other end of the string tie a magnet.
- Something to "catch"...
    — Flash Cards (on any subject)
    — Pictures of anything…fish or animals (These can be made from computer pictures, wrapping paper, old cards, magazines, or calendar pictures, etc.)
    — Something you are trying to memorize. Write either the whole thing on a note card or one word, each on a separate card. The child must "catch" the words and put them together in the correct order.

For example: | I LOVE YOU | or | I | LOVE | YOU |

Directions:

Place a paper clip on the end of each "catch." Start "fishing!"

> Kids will never even know they are practicing spelling, math facts, definitions, types of animals, etc. It is great for memorizing and learning scientific principles of magnetism as well.

THE MAGIC OF BATH TIME!

Take a giant bubble bath and extend getting clean time into play time.

Fun bath time toys
        Empty plastic food containers to pour and dip
        Kitchen strainer, funnel and plastic cups with handles
        The turkey baster is a lot of fun in the water!
        Measuring cups
        Clean sponges
        Toy boats, plastic animals and fish.

Have plenty of towels ready (line the floor outside the bathtub before you start) and don't forget to make bubble beards, mustaches and fancy hair–dos!

A plastic laundry basket works great to store toys when bath time is finished.

PRETEND...

- Pretend to be anything.

    Copy by acting out the object's motions or actions: rain, lightening, thunderstorm, a boat on the waves, melting ice, a baby bird, a kite flying, a flower bulb or seed, etc.

- Travel

    If you could go anywhere, where would it be? Why? Research that spot. What would you need to pack for that trip?

- Be a clown

    Pretend to be a clown and put on a circus performance.

- Be a magician

    Learn some magic tricks. Check out books from the library on easy magic tricks. There are lots of very easy ones that can be learned quickly. Put on shows for friends and family. Be the "before dinner" show or evening family entertainment.

    Author story: Our sons put together a great magic act. Their dad helped build props and made music tapes, I sewed costumes and drew on fake mustaches. Our eldest son did several parties for other children (his favorite was being the main attraction for his brother's fifth birthday party) and countless family shows. His favorite trick was making his brother disappear! It started with a cardboard box and eventually his dad built a wooden box painted black and decorated with gold stars. All this began with learning one trick!

- Story building

    Use a picture from a magazine, calendar or photograph and make up a story about the picture.

- Masking tape make believe

    With masking tape, make whatever shape you want on the floor and then let the imagination go from there. Below is a boat. What else could you make?
    Car, fish, house, tree, space ship, an old fashioned well, etc.

- Animals

    Pretend to be two different animals. Create a dialog between them. What would they say?

    Little children can pretend to be a lion in a cage by curling up underneath a laundry basket. Laundry baskets make great cages for stuffed animals when playing circus or pet shop.

- News reporter

    Pretend you are a news reporter and broadcast (wooden spoons make great microphones) or write a story about something that happened at home or school that day.

- Fly away…

    If you could fly, where would you go? Why? What would you see?

- The microphone please…

    Pass the wooden spoons and spatulas, use them as microphones or music director's wands and perform an impromptu concert, or radio show.

CARDBOARD BOXES

- Cardboard boxes might possibly be a child's best toy! Let children run away with their imagination. It may be just a cardboard box to you, but to a child, it may mean something altogether different! You may have gotten a new dryer…your children see a space ship in the box it came in!

    Materials needed: a large cardboard box and un-leashed imagination!

    For smaller children, create playhouses. Lay a carpet scrap or rug on the floor, hang pictures (old greeting cards, or pictures from magazines or calendars), add a mirror (foil) and together, with crayons, draw pieces of furniture inside and flowers on the outside. Cut out a window, installing a string loop for a handle or screw on old thread spools. This is one of those open-ended toys that will "grow" with your child for years. They will continue to play with this creation, only in different ways as they develop.

As children create their own imaginative toys, you become the assistant, providing the materials, extra hands, a few ideas, and a lot of communication!

A box may become something to sit or hide in, be pushed around in or become part of their "wardrobe."

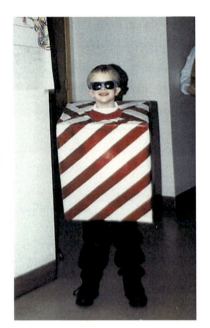

Boxes can be turned into robots or turn your child into a robot!

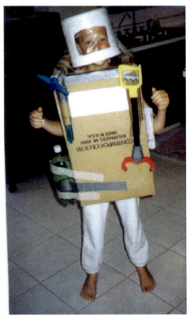

Boxes can become animal habitats…

…or made into garages, or aircraft.

You provide the supplies, extra hands, and the "oohs" and "aahs."

Don't forget the photo session!

CARDBOARD TUBES

Cardboard tubes aid in making many things. So before you throw it into the trash, have a little fun first.

What can be done with a cardboard tube?

Spy glass, binoculars, laser sword, hearing tube, tunnel for a small ball or marble to roll through (make an entire maze!) rockets, conductor's baton, relay race baton, blow a tube across the counter, insert one into the other for a telescope, etc.

Place a piece of waxed paper over the end of a tube and secure it with a rubber band. Blow through the tube. What sound does it make?

How many more uses can you find?

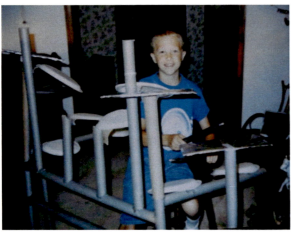
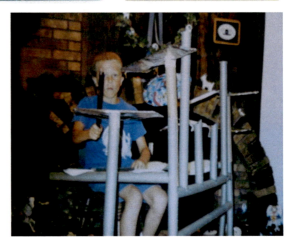

PACKING MATERIALS

"Peanuts" – besides being an excellent shock absorber in shipping, these delightful pieces of Styrofoam® can become a multitude of fun ideas. Throw handfuls of peanuts into the air creating a snow storm. Afterwards go on a scavenger hunt to find all the places they stuck during the "storm."

They make great fun floating in a sink or container of water (try to catch them with tongs).

Decorated with a magnet on the back they make adorable worms.

Paint, add glitter and use as trim on a homemade frame.

Hide a small object in a box of "peanuts." Try to find the hidden object.

Scoop them from one container to another.

Run your fingers through them!

Lots of packing paper is also fun to play in!

MILK CARTON MAGIC

Cut the bottom off of a plastic milk carton. Cartons become funnels, scoops, fish with wide mouths, and catcher's mitts for rolled up sock balls.

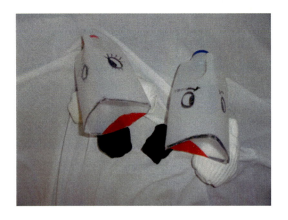

ON THE ROAD AGAIN... TRAVEL FUN!

- When traveling, let your child be the navigator. Teach them how to tell what town is next, how many miles to the next town, the population of that town. Have your child read the directions to your destination and help look for street signs.

- Count railroad cars while waiting for a train to pass. How many different kinds of railroad cars are on the train?

- Identify license plates—how many states can you find? How many from each state?

    Copy a lap size map of the United States before leaving home. Clip this onto a clipboard. Teach children how to make hash marks. Mark the state with the marks each time you see a license plate from that state. Younger children can color in the state as a license plate is spotted.

- Alphabet spy game. Follow the alphabet A to Z (omit X and Z). Players must spy an object that starts with the letter of the alphabet before going on to the next letter. You can also play this with signs. Spying a sign that has the letter you are looking for.

- Sing this modified version of an old song: "100 bottles of soda on the wall."
    "100 bottles of soda on the wall, 100 bottles of soda. Take one down, pass it around, 99 bottles of soda on the wall." Continue until there are no more bottles of soda.

- Play "Slug Bug." Each time you see a Volkswagen Beetle (or use another car like a SMART or Mini Cooper), yell out "Slug bug." The first person to find ten "Slug Bugs" calls out "Splat." (Source: Parents May 1988)

- Play "20 Questions," page 87, or "I Spy," page 86.

- Add-On-Story. Someone starts a story and then stops. The next player picks up the plot and adds to the story. Continue with several rounds of the players before stopping.

- With or without? Look for cars with or without certain things. Examples: with passengers, luggage rack, whitewall tires, people wearing glasses or sunglasses, pets, no men, no women, four doors, two doors, without a front license plate, etc.

- Count how many pickup trucks, semi trucks, green (or any color) cars, etc. within a certain time period or number of miles.

PETS!

Pets teach responsibility, commitment, unconditional love, faithfulness, the facts of life, birth and death, and how to care for illness or injury. Pets can be enjoyed by the whole family providing hours of fun and enjoyment. No matter how big or small, pets provide benefits of great value.

But, it is extremely important that if you choose to make a pet part of your family, that you research the responsibility first! To learn more about a potential pet, read books, species specific magazines, talk to a veterinarian and other people who have that type of pet, and comparison shop for the supplies, equipment, and food that the pet will need.

Reading of the material should be done by the whole family! You should discuss time, money, and responsibilities that your pet will require.

Author story: I always thought the perfect pet should live in the barn and have hooves and fur. My children gravitated towards things like hermit crabs, snakes, leopard geckos, rats (a great pet, I was so surprised!), and parakeets. All of these pets eventually lived with us and I grew to have a greater understanding and sense of enjoyment for them. These pets provided hours of fun for the whole family!

Important Parent Note Regarding Pets:

When you decide to say yes to your child's dream pet, please remember that your child is exactly that…a child. Yes, you will expect them to care for the pet, but it must be under constant supervision and direction from you, the adult.

At one point in time (and I shudder at the memory, but it was the right thing to do) we had two corn snakes, a rat and a parakeet in our kitchen/eating area. This was the place where the family spent most of our time. I could monitor the care and children's interaction with the animals to make sure it was gentle and appropriate. The animals were happier because they could see and hear us more frequently. This was especially important to our first pet rat "Popsicle Hunter." He started off in the boys' bedroom and developed diarrhea. He was moved to the kitchen (the nerve center of the home) for medical attention. He recovered quickly. We experimented with this a few times. Because rats are social animals, he was lonely in the bedroom. He spent the rest of his life, living very happily, in his activity enriched cage that sat in the corner of the kitchen. I never would have believed it before his arrival, but he was a huge source of fun and companionship.

"Popsicle Hunter" and his boy

- Plan a pet birthday party!

    A birthday party for your dog is a lot of fun. Chew sticks work great as candles in a can of dog food on a paper birthday party plate. Our dogs even wore a party hat! Sing happy birthday and give lots of hugs.

"Clifford's" birthday party

- Start an ant farm, or buy a goldfish or hermit crab.

Ant farm

Hermit crab on the stick

- Keep a journal of your pet's life.

- Write or tell a story about a pet you would like to have.

- If you were an animal, what would you be? Where would you live? What would you eat?

THE SENSES

- Name the five senses.

    Draw a picture about what you can sense with each of them.

- Create a feely box

    Directions are on page 172. Experience the sense of touch.
    Each day hide something different inside. Can you guess what it is?

- Do you hear what I hear?

    Set the timer for one minute. Sit with your eyes closed and count all the sounds you hear in that time frame. Identify the sounds. Does everyone hear the same sounds? Why do you hear more sounds with your eyes closed?

- What do you see?

    Draw a picture of what you see outside of your kitchen or bedroom window.

- Sweet, sour, salty, bitter?

    Do a taste comparison using a cookie, an orange, lemon, potato chips, pretzels or vinegar.

    Try different foods in your taste comparison.

    Taste the same foods blindfolded. Does it make a difference?

    How does the sweet of candy or granulated sugar compare to the sweet of fruits?

- The sense of smell

    How many different smells can you find in your house?

    If someone holds something under your nose when you are blindfolded, can you tell what it is? (Try a lemon, orange, apple, banana, cinnamon, vinegar, pinecones, piece of cedar wood, dirty gym shoe, etc.)

- Senses Combo

    "Paint" with shaving cream, whipped cream or pudding on a waterproof counter, table or cookie sheet. Shaving cream play is a fun way to clean off a dirty surface.

- Disability empathy

    This is a great activity to develop empathy and to talk about senses and sensitivity to other's needs.

    Have your child wear a blindfold, ear plugs, or heavy gloves for a few minutes while trying to do a simple task (listen to something you say, tie their shoes, examine a flower, drink a cup of water, watch a TV show).

    Talk about what it would be like to have a disability. What changes in their life would have to be made?

    How can they help others with disabilities? This is a great discussion starter to explore and develop values and character traits.

    Read Helen Keller's biography or about someone else who triumphed over a disability.

DISCOVERY

- Library

    Visit your local library and check out a book on a subject you are interested in. Sign up for the summer reading program.

- Color scavenger hunt

    Pick a color and see how many things you can find throughout the day or week. Compare and talk about what everyone else found at the end of the time period. Search through magazines to find pictures that are your designated color and put them in a labeled envelope. After you have done a day/week for all the primary (red, yellow, blue) and secondary (green, orange, purple) colors open your envelopes and make a rainbow collage picture.

    Make a list of twenty (pick a color) things. Pick a different color every day/week.

- Letter search

    Pick a letter and see how many times you can find things that start with that letter throughout the day or week. Find words in a magazine or newspaper that start with your designated letter, and circle them. Practice writing that letter. Find or draw pictures that start with the designated letter. Start with the letters in the child's name, or go through the alphabet.

- Hidden pictures

    Find hidden pictures on a dollar bill. How many can you find?

    Design a new kind of paper money.

- How many...
    - books do you have in your house?
    - forks or spoons are in the kitchen drawer?
    - pairs of shoes are in your family?
    - feet are in your family?
    - things can you find that are made of wood? paper? plastic?
    - steps from your bed to the refrigerator?

- Magnetic march

    Use a magnet and find what it sticks to. Does it stick to the refrigerator? Kitchen table? Research why?

- Toothpick discovery

    How many things can you do with a box of toothpicks?

    Make a square. Make an "X". How many squares or "X"'s can you make with ten toothpicks?

- Generation discovery trail

    Look at baby pictures of the children, parents, and grandparents in your family. Do any of them look alike?

    While you are looking at pictures across the generations, this is a good time to discover the similarities and differences of lives. What games did your parents or grandparents play? Do they remember a time they got in trouble? What was it for? What were the consequences? How did they celebrate holidays? What was their favorite subject in school? Did they have any pets? Did they play sports? If so, what sport? Etc.

- Tongs transfer

    You will need 2 containers, a pair of kitchen tongs and some small toys or objects. Fill one container with the small toys and objects. Let children use kitchen tongs to transfer the items from one container to another. Are some objects easier to pick up than others? Want a bigger challenge? Try picking up the objects with chop sticks!

- Magnify mania

    Explore the world around you using a magnifying glass to get a new perspective. Look at all types of surfaces, as well as people's eyes, hair, nails, plants, dirt, etc.

- Water cling

    Place a cookie sheet on a puddle of water, then try to lift it off. You will be surprised at how hard it is. The water clings to the pan creating suction.

- Strong man—pull with pulleys

    Discover how a pulley system works. Rig up a pulley (found in all sizes in the hardware department) with a small rope. Tree branches, outdoor forts or stair railing are some possible places to try your experiments. Can you lift more weight with or without a pulley?

Author Story: One day I looked outside to see my seven year old sitting on a lawn chair placed on top of the picnic table. He would pull on a rope that was flung over a tree branch running through a small pulley. As he pulled, a little platform would slowly creep up over the deck railing. I heard him giggle in delight. He jumped down and ran off the deck. In a few moments he was back pulling on the rope again. Investigation revealed a toad, fitted with a parachute on his back. The toad was hoisted up to the sky and as he jumped off, he floated back down to the ground!

PREDICTION

- Steps

    Predict how many steps it is across the kitchen or living room floor? Steps to the garage or mailbox? From your house to the corner? Walk normally to find out.

- Pairs of shoes

    Count the number of people in your family. Predict how many pairs of shoes that number of people would have. Count to see if your were right.

- Chairs

    Based on the number of rooms in your house and the number of family members, how many chairs do you think are in your house? Count them.

- Guessing game—container count

    Open a bag of jelly beans or M& M's and predict how many are in the bag as well as how many of each color. Count the candy to see if your were close. Chart this information in a bar or pie chart.

    Fill a clear jar with beans, buttons, small candies or any other small item of your choice. Guess how many are in the jar. Make it a contest with other family members. Count the items in the container to see how close you were. Take the same amount of items and put them in different size and shape containers. Does it still look like the same number of items? How does the shape and size of a container affect your perception of quantity?

- Soap boat

    Carefully carve a boat out of a bar of soap. Ivory® soap is one brand that floats well. Predict what shape and size will float the best?

OBSERVATION

- What do you see?

    Describe an object from top to bottom. Don't tell the other person what you are describing. Can they guess it from your description? Take turns. Do the descriptions differ? Why?

    Sit back to back with a partner. One person is the speaker, one is the listener. The speaker describes an object to the listener. Only the speaker can talk. The listener should draw the object as the speaker is describing their object. The listener cannot look at or talk to the speaker. How well did the speaker describe the details of the object? How did the picture turn out? What would have helped result in a better picture? Why is it important to see the person you are talking to? Why is it helpful to be able to ask questions? To get a complete picture, why is it important to get several people's perspectives?

- Have you noticed?

    How many windows or doors do you have in your house?
    How many things in your house plug in?
    Whose picture is on the one, five and twenty dollar bill?
    What picture is on a penny, nickel, dime or quarter?
    What color is the shirt your brother/sister is wearing today?
    Was your mom wearing jewelry today? What kind?
    What color is your mom/dad's eyes?
    What color hair did the check-out clerk have at the store?
    What color is your neighbor's car?
    Do you have any flowers blooming in your yard?
    Which sock or shoe do you put on first?
    If you fold your hands, which thumb do you put on top? Does your mom/dad, brother/sister have the same thumb on top?
    If you cross your legs, which leg goes over the other? Look at other people? Do they cross their legs the same as you?

    Can you think of other things?

- Magic spoon

    Make yourself turn upside down by looking into a large metal spoon. On one side you are right side up and the other side you are upside down! Older children can explore convex and concave images.

- Wave bottle

    Make a wave bottle with the recipe on page 176. Does different motion make different waves? Does the shape of the bottle affect the type of waves you can make?

- Button watch

    Is someone in the room wearing a shirt with buttons? How many buttons are on the shirt? Are they all the same shape, size and color?

COUNTING

- Count to 100 by 2's, 5's, 10's, 25's.

- Count to 10, 100, 1000.

    You decide and make the number higher as you reach each new goal.

- "This Little Piggy Went to Market" and "One, Two, Buckle my Shoe"

    Sing these familiar old tunes to smaller children to help them learn to count.
    Count fingers, toes, buttons, or peas. Anything that your children are interested in.

- People count

    Count the number of people you see in a day or on a shopping trip that are wearing glasses, black pants, earrings, a hat, etc.

- Car count

    Pick a distinguisher…color, type, style, number of doors, one license plate or two, etc.

- Counting Backwards

    Count backwards from the highest number you can count up to.
    Hop as you count. Can you count while hopping on only one foot?
    Can you count backwards when jumping rope?

- Just the Facts please!

    Write out the times tables, subtraction or addition facts.
    Make up songs to sing these facts.
    Try to accurately complete flashcards in a set amount of time. Set a timer. Try to beat your best time.

- Magic slates

    Line a sandwich container (that has an air tight lid) with a piece of black construction paper. Make it the exact same size as the bottom of the container. Pour in enough salt to just barely cover the entire bottom. Use this as a "slate" to write numbers, or math problems, When finished, just shake and start again. Mistakes don't seem as permanent when you just shake it away!

COUNT THE CHANGE

- ## Coin combinations

    Prepare a little container with a variety of different coins. How many ways can you make 25¢, 50¢ or $1.00?

- ## Random adding

    Choose three coins. How much do they add up to?
    Add a penny, nickel, dime and a quarter together. How much money do you have?

- ## Pretend shopping trip

    Go shopping with a catalog or store advertisement. Make a list writing down how much each item costs. Add up what you have spent. Older children can learn to figure percentages and add how much tax will be added to the bill.

- ## Grocery store

    Set up a pretend grocery store with real food containers or real clothes and shoes. Open cans from the bottom and reseal boxes with tape to help stock your store's shelves, or use cans and boxes from the pantry or clothes from the closet. Return the items after the store "closes" for the day. Set up a cash register with play money.

CLOCKS/TELLING TIME

- Learn to count by 15's up to 60.

- Human clock

    Stand with palms together and locked thumbs and your arms raised pointing to the ceiling above your head. This is the 12 o'clock and starting position. Swing both arms with palms still together off to one side. This is the 15 minute position. Swing arms to the floor, pointing to your feet, for 30 minutes and off to the other side for 45 minutes. Back up to the top for an hour. Chant as you swing your arms "around the clock," 15, 30 45 and hour (or 60).

- Colored face

    Help children learn to tell time by making colorful clock faces. You can use a paper clock or a real clock. Adding teaching tips to clocks with colored paper, stickers, taped on signs or dry erase markers can speed understanding of the components of telling time. To illustrate before and after concepts, divide the clock into two different colors. Use different color dry erase markers on a clock face to divide into four sections to teach quarter of an hour. Mark the minutes around the edges next to the clock numbers.

    To tell time use these prompts: First, look at the little hour hand. Second, tell the last hour. Third, look at the longest minute hand. Fourth, count by fives. Practice counting by fives and fifteens to help with reading a clock.

    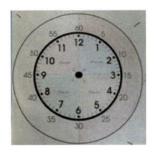  

- Important times of the day

    Draw a clock placing the hands for important times of the day. For example: wake-up, school start and finish, meal time, bed time, etc. Add pictures of that activity and post on a door or wall to help children self-regulate their usage of time.

- Add up all the numbers on the face of a clock.

    How much would that be?

FRACTIONS

- Real life fractions

    Use a real pizza, pie, cake or cookie to show fractions: ½, ¼, etc. Ask for (name a fraction) piece when serving. Present a whole food item, count the number of people you want to serve and ask how many pieces should be cut? For example: We have one pie and six people. How many pieces do we need? If only three people eat a piece of pie and we serve 3/6 of the pie, how much is left? How many sixths is that?

    Work on reductions with older children.

- Fraction teaching aids

    Use a round piece of cardboard, a picture of a pizza divided into sections and Velcro® to attach pieces to the board to make a pretend pizza. For more stability, laminate with clear contact paper before use.

    Fabric and felt can be cut to simulate a real pizza.

    Use a round stencil to make circles. Cut into different fraction pieces and label. Designate a different color for each fraction size. Laminate the pieces for longer wear. Practice using a pie tin or plate.

MEASURING

- Guess how many inches different items are. With a tape measure or ruler, measure to see if you were right. Compare and contrast sizes and see how close you can make your next prediction. If you practice, will you get better? Challenge children to use the metric system.

- Measure how tall you are. How long is your finger, arm, hand, foot, leg? How does that compare to you parents or siblings?

- Keep track of each child's height behind a door. You could use paper, or an eight foot 1x4 inch board to mark on each month.

- Guess the dimensions of your kitchen, living room, bedroom. Measure each room with a tape measure.

- Clean out the pencil container. Which one is the longest, shortest? Guess and then measure the inches.

SHAPES

- Shape search

    Look for shapes. Designate a shape for each day or week. Look for squares, circles, rectangles, triangles, octagons, hexagons, cylinders. Make the shapes harder as the children get older. How many can you find in each room? In your yard? At the store or school? In your car?

    Go through an old magazine and cut out pictures with different shapes. Categorize them into circles, squares, triangles, rectangles, octagons, hexagons, cylinders, etc.

- Shape designs

    Practice making different shapes.

    Turn shapes into people, animals or objects.

    Practice making triangles. Can you make a star out of triangles?

    Using all one shape, design a picture. Cut the shapes out of different colored construction paper or tissue paper to add color to your art.

WHERE IN THE WORLD...GEOGRAPHY

- Create a map

    Draw a floor map of your house. Label each room. Put a star on your room.
    Draw a map to your house from school or the grocery store.

- Where in the world to you live?

    Learn and write your full name, address and phone number.
    Find your city and state on a map. Put a star on the spot where you live.
    Find where your relatives live and mark their location on the map.
    What is your zip code? What are zip codes used for? Where would you find a zip code in an address?
    What country do you live in? What continent do you live on? Look at the world map and see where you live.

- How far is it?

    Using any map, attach two pieces of string to where you live. Use the string to measure the distance between two places.

- State facts

    Locate your state on the map. Read a book from the library or information on the internet about your state. What is your state bird, tree, animal, rock, motto, etc.? How many states can you find that start with the letter "M"? Pick another letter and search.

- Address book

    Make an address book of your friends and family. You can use a spiral notebook or staple single sheets of paper together. Find where the people in your address book live on a map.

- Bird's eye view

    Draw a picture that shows what a tree or your house would look like from a bird's eye view or from a satellite in space.

NEIGHBORHOOD MAP/ VEHICLE PLAY MAT

Use a piece of fabric (muslin or white cotton blend) that has been hemmed on all sides, or an old white table cloth, plain colored sheet, a clean, solid, light colored shower curtain (check your local resale shops), or a large poster board.

With fabric or permanent markers, draw your neighborhood. Label the streets and write in your neighbors' names. Label your house clearly. Draw in significant landmarks. Add trees and the family pets in your yard, if desired. Make garages and parking spots.

Make the roads the right size for small cars to drive on.

> This is a great way for your child to get to know the neighborhood, and will help if they ever get lost or need help from a neighbor. Kids love to "drive" around their own neighborhood pretending to drive by or visit the neighbors, buy gas, or shop at the stores.

WRITING

- Build a story. Make up the beginning of a story and then stop. The next person adds to the storyline from where you left off. Have fun!

- Where is your favorite place to visit? Write a poem or story about this place.

- Write a poem about something you really like.

- How many words can you think of that rhyme with cat, wet, hot, etc. Make up rhyming words.

- Write a riddle.

- Name your favorite TV shows. What do you like best about them? Older children can categorize the shows.

- Write your own TV show. What would it be about? Who would be the main characters?

- Write the days of the week. Write the months of the year. Can you say them backwards?

- Keep a journal about what is important to you, the big events of the day, the weather, etc.

- Write a letter to your grandma and/or grandpa.

- Name five animals that live in the forest, farm, desert, jungle, ocean. Pick one for each day. Read more about your favorite animals. Write a story about that animal.

- Create a book about what really scares you?

- How many words can you think of to describe the day's weather?

- Think about someone you really look up to. Design a postage stamp in their honor. Write an article that tells how you came up with the design or about that person's life.

- What are three things you would like to do when you grow up? Why? What do you have to do to achieve these goals? Write an essay about your thoughts.

LETTERS

- Magic slates. Line a sandwich container (that has an air tight lid) with a piece of black or navy construction paper. Make the construction paper the exact same size as the bottom of the container. Pour in enough salt to just barely cover the bottom of the container. Use this as a "slate" to practice letters or spelling words. When finished, just shake and start again. Mistakes don't seem as permanent when you just shake them away!

- Learn how to spell the months of the year and practice writing the names of each month.

- List all the people in your family. Now alphabetize their names.

- Create an alphabet book using names of people you know or with different animal names.

- What is the twentieth letter in the alphabet?

- Using junk mail, a magazine or newspaper, circle all the words that contain the first letter of your name.

- Using a magazine, newspaper or advertisement, find pictures that start with some blend of letters; examples: sl, st, br, bl, tr, etc.

- Write words that end in a predetermined letter. Maybe it is your name's first or last initial. Any letter can be used.

- List 10 words you can add -ing or -ed to. Rewrite the word with those endings.

- What words can you think of that do not just add the letter "s" to the end if there is more than one. For example, goose vs. geese

- How many words can you think of that end with a silent "e"?

THIS AND THAT

- What is important to you?

    Make a nametag for yourself that shows ideas of who you really are and what you think is important. Do not actually write your name on the tag. Use pictures, colored pencils, and words that describe you to make your nametag. After everyone in the family has made their nametag, lay them out on the table. Can you tell which name tag belongs to which family member?

- That's so funny!

    Learn some jokes. The library will probably have a few joke books you could check out. Practice telling a joke to someone. Make up your own knock-knock joke.

- Have a family fire drill.

    Decide on a family meeting place. Be prepared.

- Clean your room contest.

    Who can get done first? Winner gets to pick the evening family activity.

- Start a collection

    What interests you? Start a collection.

    For many years we picked up a keychain wherever we traveled. Find a creative way to display or use your collection so it can be enjoyed.

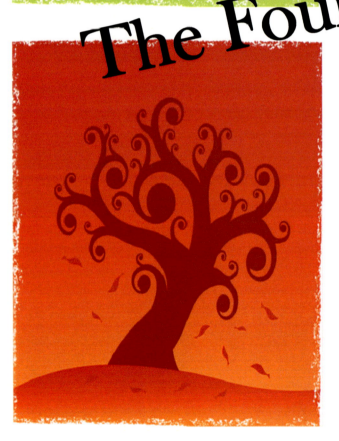

The Four Seasons

WINTER

- Make paper snowflakes.

- Build a snowman or build a snow family and pets too!

    Keep a snowman building "kit" ready for the next big, wet snow; include a scarf, hat, buttons or round rocks for eyes and mouth. Add a carrot from the refrigerator, sticks for arms and you are ready to go!

- Build a snow fort, igloo or tunnel.

    Adults should monitor this play closely. Play along with your children. It is best to play and then destroy. If left standing, melting or weak structures could collapse at a later play time.

- Have a snowball fight.

- Go sledding.

    A piece of carpet or cardboard work nicely as snow "saucers."

- Make snow angels.

- Shovel the sidewalk or driveway together as a family.

    Young children LOVE to "help" with grown-up chores. Provide a child size snow shovel and let them join in the action. Be aware that children get cold faster than adults. Monitor their temperature, make sure they stay hydrated and make sure they are dressed warm enough for the temperature.

- Indoor snow play!

    Too cold to play outside? Fill the tub or sink with snow, put on mittens, add some scoops and containers and the fun comes inside.

- Save some snow in the freezer.

    Use an airtight container or plastic bag and save some snow to play with on a hot summer day.

    Author story: One day I opened my chest freezer and it was filled to the top with snow! After questioning my preschool child, he informed me he was "saving it!". From then on we saved a controlled amount of snow in the freezer for play. It was fun to pull out a bag of snow and play with it inside the sink on days that there was no snow outside.

- Catch snowflakes on your tongue.

- Snow pictures

    Fill up an empty, clean dish detergent bottle, add some food coloring and make pictures in the snow! This idea can also decorate your snowman with a rainbow of colors.

TREATS FOR THE BIRDS

- Pine cone feeder

    Tie a piece of brightly colored yarn around the top of a pine cone. Spread peanut butter on all sides and then roll the pinecone in birdseed.

    Hang this bird feeder outside on a tree branch or garden hook and watch the birds enjoy this special treat.

- Orange half feeder

    Cut an orange in half. Scoop out the pulp for a salad or snack. Fill the skin with bird seed. Set outside on a high place.

SPRING

- Nest enhancers

    Lay out short pieces of colorful yarn somewhere in your yard. Place the yarn in an empty plastic fruit container (from the produce department or any other plastic container) and set it on top of a post or picnic table. Or you can put the yarn in a mesh bag (like oranges or potatoes come in) and hang it from a tree branch. Watch for bird nests that used your generous donation to their nest building efforts.

- Watch for baby birds.

    Observe how bird parents teach their babies to fly and eat.

- Go on a bud hunt.

    Walk around your yard, neighborhood or park and look at the different buds on the trees and plants. What do those buds look like after they open?

- Pretend to be a seed.

    Crouch down into a tight body ball. Slowly pretend to grow into whatever plant you want to be. A majestic oak tree, a beautiful rose, daisy, or carrot. Add music for a touch of drama!

- Plant a garden. Flowers or vegetables.

    Watch the growth. Older children can chart the plant growth, noting the weather conditions and daily temperatures. How many days does it take the seeds to poke up through the soil? Teach responsibility of watering and weeding.

    Author story: When our son was about three years old, he wanted his own garden. We planted five or six green bean seeds and a few flower seeds. Silk flowers were stuck in the garden spot until the seeds sprouted and came up through the soil. He faithfully watered and monitored his plants, and we got daily reports as the plants grew. He was very proud of his garden and was bursting with pride the day he harvested his green beans. We prepared them and ate them for dinner that night. We continued this tradition for quite a few years until other interests took over.

SUMMER

- Star gazing

    On a clear, warm summer night, take a blanket outside to spread on the grass. Lay back and star gaze. Can you find Venus and the Big Dipper? Read a book about stars and planets, and constellations.

- Night time sounds

    Sit outside after dark and listen to the sounds of the night. What do you hear? Can you hear crickets or frogs peeping? Night owls? Traffic sounds? Try listening with your eyes shut! Do you hear more sounds this way or with your eyes open?

- Popsicles

    Pour your favorite juice or a combination of juices into small plastic cups. Fill them about half way full, cover with a piece of foil, then add a wooden popsicle stick or a straw through a hole in the foil. The foil will hold the straw in place. Put cups on a tray and then into the freezer until frozen. Fun juice combinations: apple/grape, apple/orange, cranberry/apple.

- Fruit sparkle ice cubes

    Mix one small package of powdered drink mix with 2/3 cup of sugar and 4 cups of water. Pour into an ice cube tray and freeze. Any flavor can be used. If several flavors are made you can put one of each flavor in a glass. Then serve by pouring a lemon-lime soda over the top of the cubes. Recipe found on page 163.

- Have a watermelon seed spitting contest!

    Find a nice grassy spot to eat your watermelon slice. See who can spit the seeds the farthest!

- Shadow watching

    Find your shadow (or the shadow of your house or another object) on the sidewalk. Watch how the shadow moves, changes or disappears over time during the day.

- Sidewalk chalk

    Draw circles on the sidewalk with chalk and label them with different numbers. Have kids fill the circles with the correct number of pebbles.

    Draw a hop scotch game on a sidewalk. See page 84.

    Create pictures or games on the sidewalk or a cement pad.

- Camping

    Plan a pretend camping trip. If possible plan a real trip, even if it is in the backyard. Why not "camp" in the living room with a homemade tent? What do you need to take?

- Jump rope

    Can you jump 25, 50, or 100 times without stopping?

    What kind of rhymes can you make up as you jump?

    A childhood favorite of mine was "Blue Bells, Cockle Shells." It needs two rope turners and one jumper. Or tie one end to a stationary post. Swing the rope back and forth… not over (good for beginners), with the child hopping over the rope as it swings. "Blue bells, cockle shell, easy ivy over." At this point swing the rope over the jumper's head and continue in normal rope swings.

    Another favorite was: "Cinderella, dressed in yellow. went upstairs to kiss a 'fella, made a mistake and kissed a snake, how many doctors did it take?" Count until you mess up, then try again.

    Many other jump rope rhymes can be found on the internet.

- Fly a kite.

- Design a family flag on Flag Day (June 14).

- Play in the park.

    Don't pass by the park on the way home. Stop for a few minutes and play! Is there play equipment at the school or day care? Take a few minutes to play with your children before heading home.

- Hug a tree.

    How big around are the trees in your yard? Do your arms fit around them? Can your mom or dad fit their arms around bigger trees than the kids?

- Go on a picnic.

- Roll down a hill.

- Identify trees

    How many different kinds of trees can you find in your yard? How do they differ in leaf shape and types of bark? Do they lose their leaves in the Winter? Do the leaves change color in the Fall? What is the name of each tree? Do they live in other places in the world besides where you live?

- Climb a tree

- Earthworms

    With an adult, dig a hole in the soil and look for earthworms.
    Watch an earthworm in action. What do you think it eats?
    Investigate why worms help plants grow. Read about their important role.

- Bird watching

    This can be done at anytime of the year, but is especially fun in the Spring and Summer.

    How many different kinds of birds do you see outside today?

    Use binoculars to watch their actions. What do they eat? How do they fly? What do they sound like?

    Find the birds you see in a bird book. How and where do they nest? Do they stay in your location all year long or do they migrate? Find out what migrate means.

- Flower investigation

    Investigate the parts of a flower.

    Smell different flowers. Do they all smell the same?

    How many different colors of flowers can you find?

    Identify what flowers you have in your yard, or nearby park.

    Use a magnifying glass to get a better view of the parts of a flower or plant.

    Try putting a petal under a microscope or use a magnifying glass. What do you see?

    Draw pictures of the flowers you find.

    Keep a flower journal.

    Read a book about different kinds of flowers that live in your area.

    Take photos of the flowers you discover and keep a scrapbook.

    Pick a flower and press it between pieces of newspaper or in an old magazine, by putting several books on top of it for a few days until your flower is pressed and dried. Use your flower to make a card for someone special.

- Making an insect jar

    Empty plastic containers with screw on lids (like a peanut butter jar) with holes in the top work great for scooping up and looking at insects. An adult can make small holes in the lid by using a small drill bit.

- Insect investigation

    Draw a picture of your insect.

    Use a magnifying glass to get a close up view of the different parts of an insect. Look at the head, thorax, abdomen, legs and wings. What colors do you see? How many legs does it have?

    Journal about what you find. Where did you find it? What plant was it on? How did it act?

    Find a book that will tell you more about this insect.

- Spider web search

    Try an arachnid search. Early on a sunny morning, go for a walk around your yard looking for spider webs decorated with sparkling dew. Watch how the sun shines through the delicate webs making them look like a design of diamonds! This is also a fun Fall activity on a cool, crisp morning.

- Go on a bicycle ride!

    Ride around the block, down the street, or on a bicycle trail.

    Pull the cars out of the garage and use the garage and cement pad as a track. Can you ride around 100 times?

- Dye a flower.

    Pick white daisies or wild Queen Annie's Lace (usually found along the side of roads, in ditches, along fields or anywhere that has been left to grow wild). Fill several plastic bottles or vases with water. In each container of water add a different color of food coloring. Blue and red work well. Insert several flowers in each container of colored water and observe over the next several days. The colored water will flow up the stem and turn the veins and petals of the flower the color of the water. Very cool!

- Start a nature collection.

    Empty egg cartons are great to store a rock or shell collection. To learn more about your collection, research facts in a book or on the internet.

SAND

- Create fabulous things in the sand.

    Castles with moats, roads and cities. Use empty food containers and water to help with the shapes.

- Hand and foot prints

    Sign your name. Don't forget to take a picture. Make it a tradition to take a sand photo each summer!

- Backyard fun

    Is the beach too far away? Make a sand box in the back yard. Cover the sand to keep out unwanted cats searching for a litter box.

- Indoor play

    Want a smaller scale? Fill a box lid lined with foil, cake pan or roasting pan with sand. Place the container on a plastic covered surface (shower curtain or plastic table cloth) and play inside. Rocks, twigs, plastic animals, a bowl for water to make a lake and other items make this play time more fun. A small broom and dustpan are good to add to the end of this activity.

WATER

- Experiments

    Fill a container or sink with water. Experiment to see what sinks and what floats. Try a paperclip, rock, Styrofoam® peanut, straw, paper wad, plastic spoon, metal spoon, etc. Guess if the item will sink or float before you drop it in the water.

- Indoor water play

    Fill a sink, large container, or tub with several inches of water. Use measuring spoons, plastic cups, small plastic bowls, funnels and strainers from the kitchen or small plastic animals and fish to make play fun.

    Be sure to have plenty of towels for this play and make clean up part of the fun.

- Water play

    Enjoy the water together at a pool, lake or in your backyard. Swim, wade, float, walk and/or explore.

- Bucket fun

    No pool? Not close to a beach? A large plastic bucket filled with water can still be hours of fun on a hot day. Set it up in the grass or on the sidewalk. Grab the "toys" from the kitchen cabinet: funnel, measuring spoons and cups, strainers, small plastic bowls or empty plastic yogurt or food containers.

- Sprinkler spectacular

    Celebrate the first day of summer with a sprinkler party! If you don't have a sprinkler, hold your thumb partially over the end of a hose that has been turned on, creating small and large sprays of water. Can you hold it just right in the sun to make a rainbow?

- Water pictures

    Fill a clean, empty dish detergent (or squirt) bottle with plain water. Make water designs (art masterpieces) on the cement or the side of the house.

- Water mist fight

    When the temperatures soar, cool off by using spray bottles filled with water to have an outdoor water mist fight.

- Indoor pretend pool

    Fill the bathtub, put on your swim suits and get out the water toys! You can do this anytime of the year.

- Go fishing.

- Explore a pond.

    Use an empty white plastic food container and a small net. How much life can you find in the water? Using a white container helps you see the living organisms more clearly.

    Draw what you find.

    Identify your critters with a book about pond life.

BUBBLES

- Bubble gum

    Learn to blow bubbles with bubble gum. Whose bubble is the biggest? Lasts the longest? Who can blow and pop a bubble without it getting all over their face?

- Homemade bubbles

    Make homemade bubbles with dish detergent, water and corn syrup. The recipe is on page 170.

    Blow bubbles with a bubble wand saved from a store purchased bottle.

    See who can make the most bubbles. Whose bubble will float the longest? The highest? Who can make the tiniest bubble?

    Use string or a pipe cleaner tied in a circle to make BIG bubbles.

- Write a story about a bubble.

    What color is it? How far did it travel? What did it see on the trip?

BUTTERFLIES

- Observatory

    Research this activity first! Make a temporary observatory between your sliding glass door and screen for large insects or butterflies. Research their favorite food first. A fresh supply of food and water must be added daily. This should only be done for a few days for observation. Insects should be carefully returned to their original habitat after this time period.

- Hatch butterflies

    Conduct family research together on how to do this first! This activity must be done with much supervision, dedication, and conscientiousness.

    This idea is not new, but began in our house when my Kindergartener wanted to hatch butterflies. At the time we had a very long row of parsley growing in the garden. My son noticed that this certain caterpillar liked the parsley. He wanted to see what type of butterfly it would become. So, we made habitat buckets for the caterpillars. Sticks and a daily supply of parsley were provided to our "guests." We read books about the process of metamorphosis and planned accordingly. Every day we watched and waited. We were not disappointed. It wasn't long before we had a chrysalis. After hatching, we provided the butterflies a "half-way" house and observatory in between the screen and glass door. Fresh zinnias (their preference that we had observed) were provided daily. We hatched quite a few butterflies that year. As we released them into the wild we knew we had gained a new sense of respect and wonder about their lives.

- **Catch and release**

    Study insects, butterflies, toads, and frogs.

    Read books about your finds.

    Identify what you catch.

    Keep a journal of everything. Where you find the critter, what time of day, what plant it was by, the season of the year, the temperature outside, etc.

    Draw or take pictures of all your species.

    Use a magnifying glass to get a closer look.

    Be very gentle and release in the same spot as where you found it after investigation.

FALL/AUTUMN

- Fall leaves

    Collect pretty leaves. Sort them into piles of different shapes, sizes or colors.

    Arrange a few pretty leaves on wax paper. Cover with another sheet of wax paper the same size. Put a brown paper bag under and on top of the waxed paper while ironing with a warm iron to seal. These look pretty hanging in a window.

    Press a leaf collection in an old magazine or newspapers weighted down. When completely dry, make a set of placemats using poster board and clear contact paper. Don't forget to sign and date them. Or, make a card and send to someone special.

    Leaf Rubbings—Select a leaf that you like. Place the leaf under a piece of white paper, vein side up. Using a crayon (the side of the crayon works best) color over the leaf. An imprint of the leaf will appear. These can be cut out for decoration, used for hanging up to admire or made into a card.

- Acorn roll

    Place two to four acorns in a shallow cardboard lid, flat or shirt box. Put a piece of paper in the bottom. Add a small amount of paint about the size of a quarter (several colors are fun) on top of the paper. Drop acorns into the box on top of the paper. Hold the box and move it back and forth so the acorns roll from side to side through the paint. The acorns makes a cool design!

- Pinecone prints

    You will need finger paint in fall colors, finger paint paper or newspaper. Cover a pinecone or other large seed pod with paint. Roll it on the paper creating a design.

    The paint covered pinecones can be used as decoration after they help you paint. Let them dry, then add a ribbon or yarn hanger.

- Leaf people

    After an outdoor excursion for collection of beautiful leaves (give each child a bag to pick their favorites) come inside and make a leaf family. Arrange leaves onto paper into people shapes. Then glue the leaves down onto the paper. Markers or construction paper can be used to make eyes, nose and mouth.

- Jack-o-Lanterns

    Carve a face or design into a hollowed out pumpkin. Set a battery operated candle inside and enjoy the glow.

    Simple coloring book pictures can become designs on your pumpkin. Cut the top off of your pumpkin and clean out the seed and pulp (save the seeds to wash off, season and roast). Make a copy of your desired picture and tape it to the pumpkin side. With a tooth pick, poke holes through the paper following the outline of your picture. Remove the picture. Using a pumpkin carving knife, carefully cut out your design. Adult supervision required!

- Paper mask

    Make a mask from a larger brown paper bag. Open the bag and very carefully slip it over your head and mark the eyes, nose and mouth. Remove the bag and cut out the areas in the desired shape. Add construction paper, felt, yarn, stickers, decorations with marker or crayons to complete the mask. You can even "fringe" the bottom with scissors.

- Leaf piles

    Rake leaves into a big pile, then jump in!

    Scoop leaves up with your hands and throw them into the air making it "rain."

- Acorn hunt

    Give each child a sack or basket for an acorn hunt in the yard. After their containers are full, or the attention span has run out, put all the acorns into a cardboard box, dish pan or plastic container. Bury a small object (small ball, key, action figure, etc.). Dig through with both hands to try to find the object. Great for tactile discrimination!

- Make homemade applesauce.

    Peel, core and slice an apple for each person. Place apples in a sauce pan and add enough apple juice to just barely cover the apples. Add cinnamon, cloves and allspice to taste. (Cinnamon twice as much as cloves and allspice). Heat until tender. Mash to desired consistency. Serve hot or cold. Recipe on page 163.

NATURE ANY TIME OF THE YEAR

- Plant fruit seeds.

    Plant apple or orange seeds in a small plastic cup or in empty egg carton cups.

- Count fruit seeds.

    Predict how many seeds are in your next piece of fruit. Then as you eat the apple or orange, count how many seeds are actually inside.

- Grow hair on "Eggbert."

    Draw a face on the empty half of an egg shell. Add a little potting soil, then sprinkle a pinch of grass seed on the top. Add a gentle dusting of potting soil on top of the seed and pat gently. Keep the soil moist with water (un-softened water!). Watch your egg-man grow hair!

- Sweet potato vine

    Cut a sweet potato in half. Suspend the potato with toothpicks into a clear glass jar filled with water. Submerge the potato slightly into the water. Watch as it sprouts and grows a vine.

- Go for a walk or hike.

    It is good for your health and is fun to investigate the outdoors. You can hike in a park, nature reserve, around your block, neighborhood, in your back yard or even around and through your house!

    What surprises can you find? What types of animals, trees, flowers, insects, toads, snakes or butterflies did you see? How many people did you see?

Discovering a toad's hiding spot!

THE WEATHER

- Predictions

    Predict the weather and/or temperature for tomorrow or one day next week. Write it down and see who was the closest.

- Description

    How many words can you think of to describe today's weather?

- Charting

    The older child will enjoy charting the weather or temperature for a week, month or year, depending on interest. Take a look at the weather patterns, compare from previous years and months.

- Picture search

    Search for pictures in the clouds. Does everyone see the same thing? If you wait five minutes, will you see the same picture? What if you compare the clouds from morning to afternoon?

ARTS/CRAFTS

- Paper chains

    Use construction paper, recycled paper, computer paper, wrapping paper, store ads, comic pages, etc. to cut into strips about one inch wide and four to five inches long. The length depends on how big you want the circles. Glue or staple the strip ends together to make a circle. Interlock each new strip into the previous circle made. Continue until the chain is as long as you want.

- Book markers

    Strips of paper can also be used to create your own book marker. Add stickers, decorate with markers or crayons. Punch a hole in the top and add yarn, or ribbon. Make a bookmarker to give to a friend.

- Personalized homemade gift tags or wrapping paper

    With construction paper, wrapping paper, card stock, cookie cutters (to make different shapes), scissors, markers, stickers and creativity, make your own gift tags.

    Large sheets of plain white paper, freezer wrapping paper, newsprint, old maps or white paper tablecloths can be transformed into wrapping paper.

- Rubbings

    Under a plain piece of paper, place a flat object such as a leaf, coin, key, or cardboard cut out. Using the side of a crayon, rub over the object revealing its outline.

- Draw a cartoon.

    Color it with colored pencils. Add your own story line.

- Draw a made up creature!

- Create made up faces.

    Cut out eyes, ears, noses, mouths, and hair from magazine photos. You can even do this with animal face parts or a combination of the two. On a plain white paper plate create a face of your choice. Use glue to attach your new "face" to the paper plate. Make up a story about your new person. Attach your "face" to a popsicle stick and talk to the other children's make believe people. Put on a puppet show.

- Three-way creature creations book

    Take several sheets of plain white paper and fold them in half. Staple along the side so it looks like a book. You can add a construction paper cover if you like. Cut the pages inside into three sections. Draw a picture on each page of a person or an animal.

    You could also glue a picture of a person or an animal on each page. This can be a project that is added to each day until completed. Take turns creating different scenes by turning the three sections into three different pictures. Create a story about your new "creature."

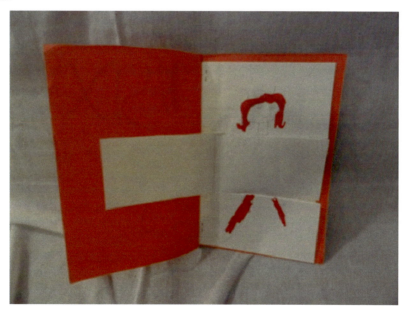

- Learn to make stick people.

    Create a stick person family. Can you draw stick animals?

- Stencils

    Use a lid from the peanut butter jar, cool whip carton or any other food container, and draw circles. Make different size circles using different size containers. Use cookie cutters to trace shapes onto lids before cutting out different shapes. Both the shape you cut out and the lid result in a stencil. A pasta measurer makes a great stencil too.

- Aluminum foil sculptures

    Tear off a piece of foil and start poking, pushing, squishing and pressing until you have the perfect piece of jewelry, animal, creature or anything your imagination comes up with!

Foil Flower   Foil Bird

- Body outlines

    Trace body outlines on the sidewalk or a large piece of paper. Decorate the outlines together.

- Fingerprint creatures

    Using an ink pad, make fingerprints on a piece of paper. Try different color ink pads. Then using a pen (or colored pencil) create people, animals, objects, monsters, etc. from the fingerprint. Let your imagination go wild.

      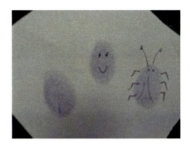

- Necklace

    String round cereals or pasta on yarn, string, ribbon, pipe cleaners or twine to make a necklace or bracelet. Create patterns and/or different color schemes.

- Collage

    Make a collage or picture frame by gluing on beans, pasta, seeds, packing peanuts, hole punch circles, etc.

    > Note: Colored pasta or rice can be used to make necklaces or collages. The recipe is on page 169. Both provide fine motor practice and the math skill of making patterns.

- Label design

    Design a label for your favorite cereal, toothpaste or hair care product. Make it completely different from the present design. Tape it onto the old container.

- Make clay sculptures. Recipe on page 171.

- Make homemade play dough.

    Recipe on page 170. Use cookie cutters, rolling pins as well as plastic scissors and knives to play.

- Surprise play dough balls

    When making homemade play dough do NOT add a color. Make the dough into white balls. Inside each ball add several drops of food coloring of your choice. As the child plays with the ball, the color is mixed. This is not good for the adult or child who has an aversion to messy hands. Keep the wet wipes handy.

- Candy cane art

    Use leftover candy canes to make hearts for Valentines' Day. Leave messages of love in crazy places for your loved ones to find.

- Play with slime or finger paint.

    These can be purchased from most discount stores…check the toy department or party favors section.

- Make silly putty—see recipe on page 171.

Miraculous Magical Moments in Minutes 159

- Fold a Fan

    Fans have been used in Japan for centuries in ceremonial dances. To make your own fan, use pretty paper or even a magazine picture that you like. Decorate the paper to make it pretty or meaningful. You could even glue lace onto the top edge. Fold the paper back and forth in half-inch wide strips so the paper becomes pleated like an accordion. Staple or tape one end together to hold your folds in place. You are ready to make a beautiful, cool breeze or perform a Japanese dance!

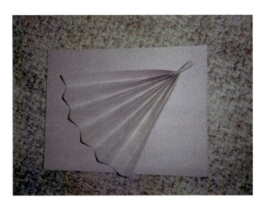

- Swirling Colors

    Use a cake pan, room temperature milk or cream, dish detergent and food coloring. Set into action a cosmic swirl of colors by adding drops of food coloring first into a pan of milk and then several drops of dish detergent. The recipe can be found on page 174. The swirling color motion may continue for several hours or even over night.

- Mix colors.

    Make new colors. Start with the primary colors (red, yellow and blue) paint. Mix two of these colors. What color does it make? Experiment with the other colors.

- Magic slates/corn syrup bags. Recipe on page 174.

    Fill a Ziploc® freezer bag half full with corn syrup and a few drops of food coloring. Seal with packing tape! Check for leaks before play!

    Use corn syrup bags as writing slates.

    Squish and make hand/finger prints.

    Hold two colors up to the light and see what color they make.

- Bleach drawing

    To do this activity wear old clothes, or an old men's dress shirt put on backwards (buttons down the back). Close adult supervision will be needed. Dip a Q-tip® into bleach (pour a small amount into the cap). Use the bleach dipped Q-tip® to draw on a piece of dark colored construction paper. Watch as your picture appears like magic!

- Marble painting

    This activity is done just like the acorn roll. Place a piece of paper in the bottom of a cardboard lid, cardboard flat or shirt box. Add a small amount of paint about the size of a quarter on top of the paper. Put a few marbles into the box on top of the paper. Hold the box and move it back and forth so the marbles roll from side to side through the paint. Several colors of paint can be used.

  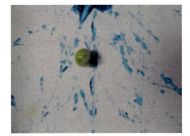

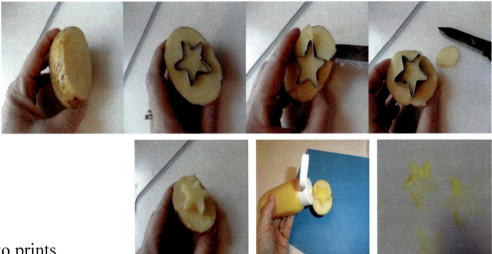

- Potato prints

    Cut a potato in half. Cut out a shape from the flat side. Cookie cutters are useful to help make a pattern. Add a large drop of paint and use the potato as a stamp on a piece of paper. Experiment with other vegetables also. How about printing with the cut off end of a stalk of celery or just one rib of celery. What design does it make?

- String painting

    Pull a string through a small amount of paint and onto paper to make designs.

- Mirror image painting

    Fold a piece of paper in half. Open the paper back up and place a small amount of paint on one side of the paper. Fold the paper in half and gently press. When you open the paper, what design did you make?

- Water colors

    Buy a box of watercolors from a discount store. Paint what you see or make up your own design. Paint on paper, coffee filters, newspaper etc.

- Coffee filter butterflies

    Paint on a round coffee filter with water colors. After you have finished painting, let the paint dry. Squeeze the filter together in the middle. Twist a pipe cleaner around to form antennae. Or, clip a clothespin over the middle, adding eyes with a marker. Attach a piece of yarn to hang your butterfly creation.

RECIPES

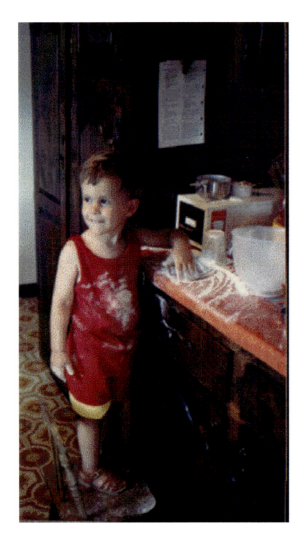

You wanted the flour where?

Anticipation…
Waiting for the cake to be done,
and watching it rise.

Is it done yet?

Fruit Sparkle Ice Cubes

Mix one small package of powdered drink mix with 2/3 cup of sugar and 4 cups of water.

Pour into an ice cube tray and freeze. Any flavor can be used.

If several flavors are made you can put one of each flavor in a glass, making it more festive.

Examples: red and green at Christmas, red for Valentine's Day, green for St. Patrick's Day, red and blue for Patriotic days, pastel colors for Spring and Easter, orange for Halloween, etc.

Serve with a lemon-lime soda poured over the top of the cubes.

Quick and Easy – One Meal's Serving
Homemade Applesauce

Peel, core and slice an apple for each person that will be at the meal.

Place prepared apples in a sauce pan and add enough apple juice to just barely cover the apples.

Add cinnamon, cloves and allspice to taste. (Cinnamon ratio should be twice as much as cloves and allspice)

Heat until tender.

Mash to desired consistency. Serve hot or cold.

Kid Friendly, Fun Food Ideas

- Hot dog buns don't always have to hug a hot dog!
  Try these fun ideas:

Wrap a cheese stick with a piece of sliced meat, add your favorite condiment, and lay it in a hot dog bun.

Spread peanut butter inside a hot dog bun or a flour tortilla and lay a banana on top. If desired, sprinkle some raisins inside before eating.

- Stuffed apple

Core an apple. Mix peanut butter, honey, and raisins together. Fill the apple with the peanut butter mixture.

- Bologna Cups

Turn a microwavable cup, measuring cup, custard cup or jelly jar upside down. Place one piece of bologna over the cup bottom (bologna should hang over the edges). Microwave 30 seconds or until the bologna forms around the bottom of the cup. Let cool slightly before filling. Fill with macaroni and cheese, scrambled eggs, baked beans, mashed potatoes with peas added for "bird's eggs," vegetables, or any other food that you desire. Bologna also curls up into a bowl if you fry it.

- Monster Toast

You will need a piece of bread, a small glass of milk colored with food coloring (in a bright color of your choice), and a small clean paintbrush. Use the milk as "paint" to create a monster on a piece of bread. Toast the bread as you normally do. Butter and eat!

Graham Cracker House

Materials: 7 graham cracker halves

Pint size empty, clean and dry cardboard carton (the size they serve milk in at schools and cafeterias or the small size that cream is packaged in at the store)

Small Styrofoam® plate

Plastic knife

Small container of icing

Decorator's bag of royal icing with round tip (icing recipe on page 167). Decorator's pastry bags and tips can be found in the cake decoration aisles at discount and craft stores.

A heavy plastic Ziploc® bag with one corner snipped off can be substituted for a pastry bag. See page 168.

Assorted cereals, colorful candies, small cookies (teddy bears or gingerbread people), mini marshmallows, etc.

Procedure:

Step #1: Place the milk carton on the Styrofoam® plate. Spread frosting on the outside of the milk carton, one side at a time. Place a graham cracker on each of the "walls." Using the decorator's bag of icing or the plastic knife with frosting, fill in the cracks at the corners of your "house." Wait a few minutes to let this dry.

Step #2: Lean two graham crackers together to make a peaked roof. Secure this with frosting. Wait about five minutes allowing the icing to harden for support. This is a good time to plan your design for the rest of the house.

Step #3: Decorate the house with candies, cereals and any other edibles. Let your imagination go wild and have fun! Remember too much weight on the roof may make it break.

Royal Icing

Ingredients: 3 Tablespoons of Meringue Powder
       (found with cake decorating supplies at discount and craft stores)
   1 pound of powdered sugar
   5-6 Tablespoons of water

Want to make only half of a recipe? Use:
   1 T + 1 ½ t. meringue powder
   2 cups of powdered sugar
   2 ½ -3 Tablespoons of water

Directions: Combine the above ingredients
   Beat 7-10 minutes at low speed with an electric mixer
   It is important to keep the icing covered with a damp cloth while working with it to prevent drying out.

Royal icing can be stored in an air tight container for up to two weeks. To re-use, beat vigorously to restore the original texture.

This icing dries very hard.   (Source: Wilton)

Another edible "glue" recipe:

Ingredients: 2 large egg whites
   1/8 teaspoon cream of tarter
   2 teaspoons of water
   3 cups of powdered sugar

Directions: With an electric mixer, beat egg whites, cream of tarter and water until foamy. Add the powdered sugar and beat on high until icing is stiff (about 5-10 minutes).

   Yield: about 1 ½ cups   (Source: Wendy, Kids' Turn Central)

Ziploc® Pastry Bag

You can make your own pastry bag using a quart size freezer bag. Fill the bag with your recipe, then using a straight edged spatula or the side of your hand push your ingredients to one corner. Cut off the tip to make an opening for the ingredients to come out. The size of the hole determines how much will come out at a one time. Start off with a very tiny snip. You can always make the hole bigger, but you cannot make it smaller once you have made your cut.

Be creative. This can be used for things other than icing. Pipe pancake shapes, or your child's initial, onto the griddle for cooking. Mashed potatoes can be made into nests and filled with vegetables or you can fill deviled eggs. Write messages with jelly on toast.

Peanut Butter Play Dough

Purpose: to create a delicious, edible modeling clay that can be eaten after you play! This is a great snack time activity!

Materials:
    2 cups of smooth peanut butter
    ¾ cup honey
    2-3 cups powdered milk (enough to keep the mixture from being sticky)
    Large mixing bowl and spoon

Procedure: Combine the ingredients together in the mixing bowl until the consistency feels like modeling clay. Turn the dough out onto a CLEAN surface and knead until smooth.

Playtime! Give each child a ball of "clay" and let them create. Make sure hands and surfaces have been thoroughly cleaned before this activity! After each creation has been admired, eat away!

How to Color Rice and Pasta

Materials:
    Pasta or Rice (depending on your project)
    Gallon Ziploc Bag
    Rubbing Alcohol ¼ cup for every cup of pasta or rice
    Food Coloring
    Newspaper

Procedure: Protect your work surface with newspaper or an old paper tablecloth (from the party store or left over from a party). Add rubbing alcohol and desired color into a Ziploc® bag. Seal the bag and mix the coloring with the alcohol. Add coloring until desired shade is obtained. Open the bag and add pasta or rice. Reseal bag and shake or move the pasta/rice around until completely coated with color. Lay flat, still inside the bag, turning every 30 minutes for several hours (until the desired darkness of color is achieved). The longer you let it sit, the deeper and more vibrant the color becomes. Drain the alcohol from the bag and spread the pasta out on newspaper or a cookie sheet to dry. Dry over night. Store in air tight containers for use in projects.
Caution! Food coloring will stain your hands and clothes.

Bubbles

Materials: 2 cups of dish detergent
Dawn and Joy work well
6 cups water
¾ cup corn syrup
1 gallon container – clean, empty milk carton

Procedure: Mix the above ingredients diluting with more water if needed.
For best results, mix the night before or let the mixture sit for 4 hours before use.

Fun Ideas: Try blowing bubbles with a bent wire hanger, pipe cleaner or string circles. Use a kids pool to make a giant bubble solution container.

Save the wands from the store bought bubble containers and reuse. See who can blow the biggest bubble, the tiniest bubble. See whose bubble lasts the longest, floats the highest, travels the farthest.

Play Dough

Materials: 2 cups flour
1 cup salt
3 teaspoons cream of tarter
1 tablespoons vegetable oil
2 cups water
food coloring
Dry powered drink mix, if desired, for smell
> Keep in mind…the color of the drink powder will mix with the food coloring creating a new color. For example, if you add blue coloring to a red drink mix, your dough will turn out a shade of purple.

> Glitter, if desired Note: may be added after heating, before kneading. This is best if NOT used with flavoring, in case the play dough is accidentally tasted.

Procedures: In an UNHEATED electric skillet, mix the above ingredients in the order listed, stirring after each addition. Heat the skillet to 350 degrees Fahrenheit. Stir mixture until set (no more gooey spots). Make sure you cook it long enough. Take dough out of skillet and knead (like bread dough…fold, push, turn) until mixture is smooth and pliable. Using rubber gloves helps handle the hot mixture. Store in air tight container. This keeps several months.

Silly Putty

Materials: 2 parts white glue
             1 part Sta-Flo liquid starch

Procedures:
Combine the ingredients in a bowl and stir until thickened. Knead (as you would for bread) on a clean surface until completely mixed. Mixture should be solid, but not stretchy. Adjust amounts as necessary. Let the putty dry a bit before it is workable.

Store in an airtight container.

To blow bubbles: Lay silly putty flat on a clean surface. Fold the silly putty over in half and seal it on the edges, like a tart. Insert a straw and blow bubbles! This works best if you have played with the silly putty first.

Source: Recipes for Fun! Child Care Resource and Referral Kalamazoo Regional 4-C

Cornstarch Clay

Materials: 1 cup cornstarch
             2 cups baking soda
             1 ¼ cup cold water

Procedures:
Stir the ingredients over medium heat for about 4 minutes. The mixture should thicken to mashed potato consistency. Remove from the heat and turn onto a plate. Cover the clay with a damp cloth until it is cool enough to handle. Knead as you would bread dough. Mixture is very soft and smooth. It will dry out and be white.

Store in an air tight container or form the clay into whatever shape you desire. Let it air dry until hard. You sculpture may be painted after it hardens, if desired.

Source: Recipes for Fun! Child Care Resource and Referral Kalamazoo Regional 4-C

Feely Box

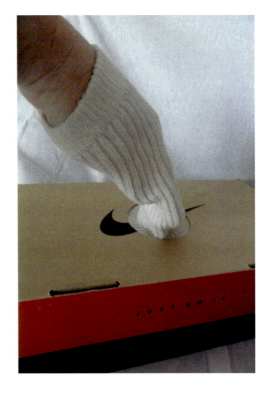
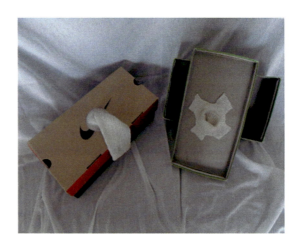

Materials: A container: shoe box, or plastic soda bottle with the top half cut off
One sock: large enough for an adult hand to go through.
Hot glue gun
Scissors

Procedure: Cut off the top of the sock

If using a coffee can or soda bottle – pull the sock top over the bottle and hot glue in place or use strong strapping tape.

If using a shoe box — cut a round hole in the middle of the box (a lid or glass make a nice stencil) Insert the raw edge of the sock through the hole. Cut four tiny slits on the raw edge of the sock so it will lay flat. Glue the raw edge of the sock to the underside of the lid. Let dry before use.

Tips: Experience the sense of touch.
Hide items in the box and let children guess what is inside.

Newspaper Hat or Boat

Materials: One piece of 8 ½ x 11 paper or a sheet of newspaper folded in half along the center fold, scotch tape.

Newspaper is best for hats. Copy paper is best for boats.

Procedure:
Decorate your paper however you wish, then fold following the following diagrams and instructions below.

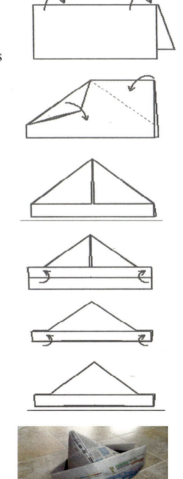

1. Fold a sheet of newspaper in half along the center fold, or, fold an 8 ½ inch piece of paper in half by folding the 8 ½ inch sides together. The fold should be at the top.

2. Both top corners should be folded down towards the center of the paper.

3. After the corners have been finished the paper is in the shape of a triangle.

4. The front bottom flap should be lifted and folded up.

5. Repeat this on the other side.

6. Secure your folds in place with scotch tape.

The finished project can be worn as a hat or set on top of the water for a short float! Floating works best with paper rather than newsprint which is absorbent.

Swirling Colors

Materials:
- Low dish or pan
- Milk (at least 2%, or cream) at room temperature
- food coloring
- dish soap (Palmolive and Dawn work well)

Procedure:
Pour milk into the pan until about ¼ to ½ full. Add food coloring (several drops of each color) onto the top of the milk. Put a few drops of dish detergent along the edges of the inside of the pan. Watch the colors begin to move.

Tips: The milk MUST be at room temperature in order for the movement to go quickly and wide spread. If the pan gets bumped, it may stop the motion. If it stops, try adding a little more soap. Watch it over night. What happens?

Magic Slates

Materials:
- Heavy duty storage bags that seal. **Check each bag before you start to see if it has any leaks in the corners.**
- Corn syrup
- food coloring
- clear, wide plastic tape

Procedures: Pour about 1/3 cup of corn syrup with a few drops of food coloring into each bag. Primary colors work well, especially if using for how colors are made. (Red + Yellow = Orange; Red + Blue = Violet; Yellow + Blue = Green) Seal each bag and add a reinforcement of clear packing tape across the top to prevent curiosity sticky messes!

Tips: Children love to squish, manipulate, draw numbers/letters and hold up to the light blending two colors. Always check the bags for leaks before and after each play time!

Erupting Volcanoes

Purpose: To simulate a volcanic eruption

Materials: small cap or lid (syrup cap, soda bottle lid, etc)
container: pie tin or baking pan
1 tablespoon baking soda
1 tablespoon vinegar
red (or your choice) food coloring, optional

Procedure:
1. Place baking soda in the cap/lid
2. Color vinegar with food coloring
3. Put the lid inside the container
4. Pour vinegar solution into the cap

Results: Foam bubbles over the top and down the sides of the lid.

Why? The baking soda reacts with the vinegar producing carbon dioxide gas. The gas builds up enough pressure to force the liquid out the top of the container. The mixture of gas with the liquid produces the foam. Amounts of baking soda and vinegar can be increased as desired, after you have experimented.

Variations: It is also fun to put baking soda in a soda bottle. Add the vinegar and quickly slip a balloon over the top. The balloon will expand with the gases given off from the chemical reaction.

This concept can also be done with yeast, a soda bottle, and room temperature water. The reaction will take longer however. Results can be monitored and/or charted over the days. The gases produced by the yeast are what cause bread to rise in the baking process.

Wave Bottles

Materials: Clean empty plastic bottle. A smooth sided bottle works best.
             Water
             Mineral oil, Vegetable oil, or Baby oil
             Quick bonding glue
             Optional: glitter, sequins, "jewels", crayon shavings, beads

Procedure: 1. Fill the clean bottle with water about one third to one half full.
             2. Add a few drops of food coloring and if desired the optional materials.
             3. Fill the rest of the bottle with oil.
             4. Glue the cap securely onto the bottle by applying the glue to the inside of the bottle cap and screwing it on.

Tips: Gently move or roll the bottle back and forth to produce waves.
        Shaking the bottle too hard will prevent waves from forming.

You have just explored more than 500 ideas! These are only a few children's activities. There are many more!

I hope this will be a spring board for you to try other activities. Here is some space to add your ideas. Custom design activities around your own family's interests, values, skills and talents. Have fun!

Ideas:

Resources

The following books are recommended for further reading on this subject.

1. Hilton, Joni (1992) <u>Five-Minute Miracles 373 Quick Daily Projects for You and Your Kids to Share</u>. Philadelphia: Running Press.

2. Lansky, Vicki (1988) <u>101 Ways to Tell Your Child "I Love You"</u>. Chicago: Contemporary Books

3. Newman, Susan (1993) <u>Little Things Long Remembered Making Your Children Feel Special Every Day</u>. New York: Crown Publishers, Inc.

Developing a patchwork of miraculous memories is simple!

Remember…every day items that surround you holds the potential to be a prop, or supply an imaginative idea, creating a magical moment.

Epilogue

My mother inspired me as a child to be creative. She can see beauty in everything, can turn anything into something creative; and, always finds something positive in every situation!

It was Mom who taught me to "waste not, want not;" and, the word "bored" was not allowed in my home growing up. Whatever the situation, mom could "whip-up" something to play and have fun with. It generally revolved around her endless work, but I never noticed due to the *magical moments* she inspired. The paraffin from the tops of our homemade jelly were warmed and fashioned into roses, a single remaining earring became decoration on a doll's dress, under the pine tree became a place where the fairies played, card tables became houses, clothes lines turned into tents, clothespins sprang alive into people, boxes were turned into amazing uses and the list goes on and on...

A Special Thank You...

To my husband who wears many "hats": best friend, confidant, encourager, soul mate, advisor, business manager, and editor. He believes I can do anything; and is always there to support, lending a helping hand in whatever idea that I become passionate about!

To Jessica and Dana who did the first edit and gave me a realistic view of this project. To Heather who contributed in part her graphic design skills; and, to Dottie, a special friend who devoted countless hours helping with formatting, editing, and assistance in launching this project, and provided an endless supply of prayer and encouragement.

To my son who supplied formatting and printing guidance.

To my family and friends for their encouragement and prayers.

The gift of these people is a special blessing for which I am so thankful. Without them, the dream of this book would not have developed into reality.

"Plans fail for lack of counsel, but with many advisors they succeed." Proverbs 15:22
Holy Bible, New International Version

About the Author

Becky Baxa is a wife, mom and grandma. She has been a certified teacher for thirty one years.

She has a Bachelor's Degree in Home Economics Education from the University of Illinois and a Master's Degree from Iowa State University in Family and Consumer Sciences Education and Studies.

A Patchwork of opportunities and experiences has been bestowed upon Becky as she moved throughout the Midwest with her husband's job transfers. During the creation of what Becky fondly refers to as her life's "crazy quilt," she has experienced a wide variety of, and often unexpected but amazing, experiences.

Her "quilt blocks" include: Christian Education, Sunday School Coordinator, Public High School Teacher, Education Coordinator, Trainer for Licensed Child Care Providers, Cable Access Show Developer and host of the show <u>Child Care Futures</u>, Developer of State Curriculum video series for Child Care Providers, Preschool Teacher, Staff Development Contractual Trainer, Conference and Workshop speaker, Substitute Teacher, Home Bound Instructor, Teacher Naturalist, Cake Decorator, Dairy Goat Breeder, and Prison Ministry Volunteer.

Life Theme:

"Whatever your hand finds to do, do it with all your might."
Ecclesiastes 9:10

Holy Bible, New International Version